Ghosts of the High Desert

GIOVANNA BLACK

BALBOA.
PRESS

A DIVISION OF HAY HOUSE

Balboa Press books may be ordered through booksellers or by contacting:

Balboa Press
A Division of Hay House
1663 Liberty Drive
Bloomington, IN 47403
www.balboapress.com
1 (877) 407-4847

Because of the dynamic nature of the Internet, any web addresses or links contained in this book may have changed since publication and may no longer be valid. The views expressed in this work are solely those of the author and do not necessarily reflect the views of the publisher, and the publisher hereby disclaims any responsibility for them.

The author of this book does not dispense medical advice or prescribe the use of any technique as a form of treatment for physical, emotional, or medical problems without the advice of a physician, either directly or indirectly. The intent of the author is only to offer information of a general nature to help you in your quest for emotional and spiritual well-being. In the event you use any of the information in this book for yourself, which is your constitutional right, the author and the publisher assume no responsibility for your actions.

Any people depicted in stock imagery provided by Thinkstock are models, and such images are being used for illustrative purposes only.
Certain stock imagery © Thinkstock.

Print information available on the last page.

ISBN: 978-1-5043-4661-0 (sc)
ISBN: 978-1-5043-4662-7 (e)

Balboa Press rev. date: 11/30/2015

Written by Giovanna Black

Dedicated to: Ms. Johnson my 7th grade teacher who in middle school asked me to give her an autographed copy of my first book. This is for you. And last but not least, my family and friends. You know who you are and I love you much. Namaste.

1

The light was gone but perhaps it would return now that the darkness was over. At the time I had just graduated from a private Christian high school set in the suburbs of Southern California. It is there that heaven and hell existed on a daily basis; five days of the week, from 8am to 2:45pm. Hell was being in a constant state of discomfort knowing one did not fit in and heaven was well…I had not found that yet.

Some may wonder; how can a Christian school be hell? Isn't that some kind of paradox? Perhaps these days a hellish Christian school is not such a paradox anymore considering the large array of church scandals and other kinds of trauma stemming from organized radical religion. Religious Trauma. Everyday I was made by the students to feel "less than" and "the other." I never learned how to listen to my angels from church, or from chapel every week at the school. Instead I learned from them how to see and struggle with my demons, which made me sink deeper and deeper into a hole of darkness.

"Giovanna! Honey, it's time to go!" I turned around and saw my Mum with her light taupe skin waving to me from her little car she affectionately called 'the Shoe.' With my High School diploma in hand, I turned my back on hell and walked towards my freedom. As I climbed into the air-conditioned car I glanced one last time at the building that represented years of agony and I mouthed a silent, "Fuck you." Instantly I felt immature and scrambled to find something positive I learned from being in a private Christian School. I often try to see the light in dark moments, but Lord knows that this time there was no light.

Then the Fall came quickly after graduation. I clutched tightly my bags full of clothing, books, and other objects I held dear. I said good-bye to my father and sisters and although I love them I felt nothing. No ting of sadness seeped up, no tightness of the throat threatened to cut off my breathing. It was a strange feeling. *Hmm…perhaps because I am finally content? I am finally off to college as a freshman fresh out of high school.* I survived a dark hole. So perhaps I endured hell to reach soon to be heaven? The possibilities were exciting, because I knew any place had to be better than High School. Any place was better than being on the brink of death. I tasted the future I previously thought I would never see. Like a small sample of chocolate that leaves you wanting more.

Once again I slipped into the Shoe with Mum and waved bye to my father standing proud and smiling big. His dark brown skin glowed in the sun as he stood by my two sisters. My sisters were smiling as well and I knew I would miss them. They were my best friends, my companions, my partners in crime, and my therapists. I hoped as we drove away that they would not forget me. I did not want to be a ghost that they vaguely remembered once in a while. Call it Middle Child Syndrome or the ego if you will, but don't we all have a need and desire to be remembered? Who wants to be forgotten? I think it is that eternity within us all; we forget our Source is endless and fight to be known.

"This is exciting huh?" My mother smiled warmly at me as we passed the 101 freeway. I nodded and smiled in response trying to push down the lump that had now come alive in my throat and threatened to incite a waterfall of tears. I would miss her warmth and my father's security…which was always weird considering the deep conflicts I had with him. I would miss my sisters' love and their mere presence. I looked away and pretended to be preoccupied with taking in the scenery as we drove to my soon to be dorm. Like most present mothers-she noticed my futile attempt to act like, "It's all good." She tapped me on my shoulder and when I made eye contact with her so that I could read her lips she said, "It's ok to be nervous, it's gonna be a big change. But remember your canvas is blank-you can paint it any color you want so embrace the experience." I smiled wearily and took in every word she said as if I was in a desert, and her words were the last drop of water I had left to save my life. I imagined her words being carved onto my soul so that they could keep me going when I need it most.

2

We arrived. The dorm buildings were beautiful and had an artistic flair to them. In me a small surge of curiosity and anticipation popped up for a second. After we got everything unpacked and settled into my room, Mum gave me a tight hug and waved bye. "I love you," she signed as she drove away and I stood on the curb a while. "Hmm…maybe I will be ok," I mused. I looked up and noticed the sky was a beautiful blue-like Costa Rica's ocean. I smiled. One thing I would always be thankful for was my mother's installation of fierce independence in us. Because of that I could take unfamiliar situations and make them as comfortable as possible. A part of me wished she stayed longer, just to help me ride out the awkwardness of a new place and city. I started to ponder about her childhood and all that she survived, and thought maybe she wanted to be sure her daughters could always face life head on if no one is around to buffer the pains. I begin to overanalyze way too much, but one thing Mum always said; "You come from my family, we're a family of thinkers. It's a good thing."

I plopped down unto my dorm bed and observed my now furnished and decorated side of the room. My imagination began to run wild with all kinds of crazy things that could happen in the next few hours. What if my roommate turned out to be a serial killer and tried to kill me in my sleep? Or maybe she would be prettier than me and get all the guys I wanted? I turned onto my side and looked at the empty space where a stranger will soon be residing with me for a full year. A full year-how the heck will I survive? This is when being a "thinker" gets me in trouble-creating worst case scenarios that most likely will never happen. I fell asleep and put my imagination to rest for a bit.

After a couple hours I opened my eyes slowly and almost forgot where I was. I sat up quickly and slipped off the bed just as my roommate entered the room. I did a quick sweep of her and the room. She was tall and had straight, dark brown hair that hung just above her shoulders. She was pretty much to my dismay-but her energy was pleasant so I decided to check my insecurities about my own appearance at the door.

"Hey there, I'm Pillar," She smiled and extended her hand.

"Nice to meet you, I'm Giovanna." I shook her hand.

"That's an interesting name-are you Spanish?" She asked. Inside I was rolling my eyes at the assumption that I must be Spanish because of my peculiar appearance and name.

"No, I am not." I responded as politely as I could. Confusion replaced Pillar's smile. I smirked with the satisfaction of knowing I had confused her with my answer, and I was determined to leave her guessing my nationality. In typical Gemini fashion the other side of me began to feel guilty for not clarifying my racial/ethnic identity. After all, this would have been a perfect opportunity to educate another person about race; the multicultural population, not making assumptions, and how society puts labels on people to quell their own discomfort in "not knowing." I never felt like a "confused mulatto" growing up. The only time I felt I had to define myself was when other people asked me to, or to quell their confusion and curiosity.

"So…where you from?" I asked her in an attempt to fill the awkward silence that ensued.

"Here in California-born and raised. You?"

"Same here." I smiled. Two native Californians. *Hmmm…we could be very good friends.*

That night we checked out the cafeteria near our dorm and met some pretty cool people. I was loving it. After years in school struggling to read lips and knowing I did not belong 100% in any crowd for countless reasons, this was a welcomed change. All around me there were pockets of hearing and deaf people communicating via ASL and the diversity was amazing. No one was shunning me, no one was making fun of my awkward puberty phases, no stuck up rich racists reading "Mein Kef" in front of me were making me feel inferior. No one was complaining about how "Black people get away with everything," while I sat in class boiling and trying to calmly explain history to no avail. It was as if some spirit had pulled me up from drowning in the hole, and was gently pumping life into me. I could breathe a little easier now.

Despite all the relief and joy I felt, the darkness still followed me like a ghost who will not go to the light. I was not exactly sure why, although I did have some hunches. After years of trauma and religious brainwashing, it was hard for me to hear that small voice inside. So maybe I feared I had killed the voice and could no longer follow my own beating heart.

3

A few months had passed and I was feeling at home in college. I visited my family a couple times and was glad to see them each time. However, nothing beat living in the dorm and having utter freedom to come and go as I pleased and not having to hide my whereabouts. The only thing I had to hide was the fact I was not yet 21 years old. My friends and I had to rely on the "older" students to get Smirnoff or tequila for us. Either that or we had to attend various parties where we knew free drinks were in abundance...usually keg parties As hard as I tried when I was 15 years old to get drunk at my then best friend's place-I could not. I downed tequila shots non-stop and to my surprise, and perhaps relief, I did not feel the affects of drunkenness take over me. For that reason, during college I felt confident every time I had a drink. As if having a plastic cup in my hand that wreaked havoc on my organs meant that I was "the shit" and made me more attractive. No wonder one person I knew called this addicting toxin "liquid courage."

I remember one night when I was 15 years old, my best friend and I went over to hang with a group of 20 year olds. We all had tequila shots, and my friend was very drunk. It was the first time I had witnessed a person under the influence. She began to cry and scream, "I'm so drunk! My mama's gonna kill me! Nooo!!" And then she ran out the front door and proceeded to continue running down the nighttime streets. The boys and I were dumbfounded and a bit amused. I ran after her and summoned her to come back to the house and sleep it off. After about 3 tries, I was successful. I do not remember much after that. Those teenage years were full of grief, amusement, and close calls.

During one of those keg parties, with my "liquid courage" in hand, I made eye contact with this guy. His name was Jimmy. He was a dream; tall, dark, and had a smile that could make any girl putty in his hands. When he flashed that smile directly at me I tried my best to act interested but not too interested. "Shit, do I look desperate?" I muttered under my breath and tried to look more indifferent to his gaze…but not too indifferent. Damn I'm confused. As I was trying to rebalance my Gemini soul Jimmy walked up to me.

"So what's up?" He grinned

"Oh-nothing much. Just chilling." I responded nonchalantly and flipped my spirally curly brown hair over my shoulder.

"Want another drink?" He asked. "Yeah sure." I gave my best sexy-but-not-too-sexy smile. Jimmy took my hand and we walked over to the beer keg. I watched as he pumped the keg and I drooled as I saw traces of the muscles in his arm twitch. He handed me my freshly filled cup. "Thanks" I giggled.

Then that's when it happened-he leaned in and kissed me. We made out for hours with no regard for anyone that had to witness our inability to control hormones. Hey, what to do? I was putty in his hands.

The next morning at the cafeteria Pillar asked me what had happened with Jimmy. She heard through the deaf vine that we had hooked up and had sex on the old plaid couch at the party, then broke two windows in the frat house for fun. "What the fuck?? Who said we di that??" My mouth dropped at this outlandish rumor that spun out of control quicker than a forest on fire during the Santa Ana Winds season in California. It was like being back in High School again surrounded by immaturity. "Jasmine told everyone she saw you two…so it's not true?" She trailed off. "God no! I'm still a virgin." I blurted out. *Jasmine-fucking toxic.* It is hard to remember that those who spread rumors, or try to destroy other people, often need help the most. Something in them is spewing damaging fumes from a neglected wound. Pillar choked on her orange juice, "You are a virgin?" She was gawking at me as if I said my birthplace is Venus and I would like to return there as soon as possible. "So? What's wrong with that?" I inquired narrowing my eyes. "Nothing, it's just that you seem so-" She broke off unsure of what to say without offending me further.

"I am open and comfortable with sex, but I just rather save the "whole thing" for when I meet someone I'm comfortable with and that I trust. I'm not trying to get pregnant either you know. I have dreams." I explained eating my dry French Toast that no amount of artificial syrup could moisten.

"Oh, ok cool. Well I respect that you were able to wait for so long," Pillar shrugged, "Anyway, let's go before we're late to class," She said hurriedly before I had a chance to ask her what her first time having sex was like. A part of me sensed she would not want me to know. My stomach cringed. The feeling was familiar, although I could not pinpoint why.

I had a brief flashback to when I was in HS and would sneak out with my friends to go over to random guys homes. We lied about our age, so we ended up with guys who were well over 18 years old. The oldest was in his 30s and was disgusting-he had 2 missing teeth. My stomach churned at the memory of him trying to kiss me and pull down my pants. I pushed him away and he thankfully left me alone eventually. Then I remembered when I was 11 or 12 having the same experience with a much older man. And then there was that nightmare I always have involving me trying to fight my father. *God. I feel gross.* I shook my head as if that'd make the memories fall out of my brain and wither on the ground to never come back up again. I went back to my dorm room and pulled out my purple journal and decided to write something positive, hoping it would seep into my hands and into my being somehow;

"The sun arrives
See the dawn, right before my eyes
So then we go
Trying to survive
Maneuvering this crazy life
But he shows me the beauty so
That it's alright
The shadows still sleep with me
Quietly like ghosts next to me
But you bring sunshine
Even at the nighttime."

4

I could not focus in Psychology class. Not just because of the fact that our professor was hot, but also because I wondered, "Am I being stupid waiting this long to have sex with someone?" "Why don't I just get it over with?" No. I made a decision and this is the only thing I have control over in my life since other parts of me had been damaged, so this was all I had left. Therefore, I will have control over who I decide to open my legs to. That was that I decided and felt sort of content once again. During class I scribbled in my notebook since a poem came to me. I was always thinking of creative verses for poems at the most random moments.

"The light keeps coming
The sun keeps blinding
My heart won't stop beating
And my heart keeps soaring
It's holding me
And keeping me a prisoner of hope."

After my last class I received a text from Jimmy just as I exited the classroom and said bye to Pillar. He wanted to meet up for a last minute meal to which I eagerly obliged. There was no time to run back to my dorm and freshen up. My curly hair was even more wild than normal due to not bothering to fix it this morning. I now regretted choosing to hit the snooze button rather than use that 30 minutes to at least spray some conditioner water on my Medusa hair. Sigh. Oh well, I convinced myself if he really liked me then he would see past my "just-woke-up" appearance and focus on my soul. Ha. I chuckled. Who was I kidding? Since I was a little girl I had convinced myself that all straight boys and men are the same-they cannot see the soul I wrongly believed. I texted Jimmy back and agreed to meet him soon.

I walked up to the place he wanted to meet at. And there he was, a beautiful vision, sitting on the bench in front of a hotdog place. *Fuck. I am a vegetarian.* "Hey beautiful," he flashed his smile as he walked up to greet me. We hugged and I just wanted to linger there, feeling his arms around me. "Sorry, I look like a mess right now," I touched my hair apologetically. "What? You look beautiful as always," he replied and gently tugged on one of my frizzy curls. I melted when he touched me. "These are the best hotdogs-you'll like them," he said taking my hand once again. This time, instead of liquid courage in my hand, I had what felt like a pound of flesh from some poor animal. I winced and tried my best to put on a poker face. I did not want to ruin my chance of us going out again, so I sat down on the bench and took a bite. I pretended to love it. "It's great huh? Could eat this everyday," Jimmy said through mouthfuls of pig…god…what if they used a baby pig to make this? I tried to erase the thoughts of PETA and animal documentaries from my mind and focus on what he was saying. One cannot read beautiful chocolate raspberry colored lips and fake liking meat at the same time.

"So you're mixed aren't you?" He inquired. "Yep, my Mum is white-German and Swiss and so on. My father's ancestors were from Ghana and his mother was a mix of Blackfoot Nation." "Ooo that's hot," he drooled. That was always a turn off when men became enthralled by my multiracial heritage. It made me feel like a lab rat and that I had nothing else to offer but to stand in a cage all day being examined and prodded with curiosity. I decided to let it go. Later I could try to educate him and all that stuff that comes along with being a woman of color. Happy to oblige, but wish people would educate themselves first instead of "innocently" offending me.

After two hours of witty conversation and much laughter, we walked back to the dorms. He dropped me off at my dorm first and we of course kissed. His lips were full and smooth

Lord, so soft. "Wanna go to my dorm?" He whispered. "Yes I do!!" I wanted to scream, but instead I whispered back, "I can't. I'm not ready for that yet." *Oh my god.* I felt like an idiot after the words spilled out of my mouth. They made me sound like one of those naïve, born again Christians who save their selves for marriage, because they were taught by perverted, power hungry males…usually straight white males… that sex is the devil. I shifted uncomfortably on my feet as I waited for his reaction. "Oh, alright. Well, ummm…I guess I'll text you then." And there he went. Walked down the hall and exited my dorm building as if I told him I have an STD and would like to give him one.

I don't need him. I convinced myself and crawled into bed. I didn't bother changing out of my clothes and fell asleep as soon as my eyes closed. The loneliness did come again. It always does. No matter how often I tried to convince myself everyday and night that I don't need anyone to hold me or be there to tell me it's ok. *That's stuff for corn dogs, wimps, and people with no self-control.* Yeah-I told myself that even though I knew even while dreaming that it was not true. The darkness was not friendly to me. The nightmares that came with it were constantly trying to wake me up to reality. If only I had known I could face that darkness with all the light that existed in the world.

5

When I woke up the next morning to the vibrations of my alarm, I noticed that Pillar had not slept in her bed. She was nowhere to be found. I walked and stumbled half asleep into the living room and kitchen. Nothing. Thank God it was Friday-no classes today. I wrapped my bed sheet around my shoulders and walked heavy-footed back to my room and picked up my phone. *"Everything ok?"* I typed to Pillar. A few minutes later my phone vibrated and her message came through, *"Wink wink. Met a guy last night."* *"Lol, looking forward to hearing about it,"* I messaged back. I laid down on my bed and closed my eyes while waiting for Pillar. I had not slept well last night due to the usual nightmares of him attacking me. I never gave them much thought. I just assumed they were my brain running haywire and trying to make sense of my anger. It fluttered softly everyday like a tiny-lit candle, but at night when I slept it exploded and roared into a firestorm. I wrote in my journal;

> "Life was a gift
> And I lived it well
> I took the sourness
> And made it the sweetest."

When Pillar returned to our dorm later that day, we smoked weed all evening in our room. We put towels under the closed door to keep the sage-like smoke from escaping into the hall and reaching the nose of angry Residential Advisors with no life. Pillar had some good connections for weed, so we were in constant supply. "I think I like him," she slowly exhaled the delicious smoke, "but he's a player." Her story was the same as any college student; girl meets boy, boy and girl hook up, girl on Cloud 9, boy has other girls lined up, girl still can't stay away. "So what happened with Jimmy?" She passed me the pipe and looked eagerly at me, obviously hoping for a juicy romance story. I told her what happened, starting with my unkempt appearance, the un-vegetarian meal, and provided every other detail. Pillar burst out laughing when I got to the end. "He walked away?" She guffawed. "Umm…it's not *that* funny," I could feel my face burning with embarrassment.

"No, no. You're right. It is not funny, Gia. It's just…" She trailed off leaving me with no explanation for her sudden need to laugh at my ability to scare away a guy in less than 24 hours. "Look. It's his loss if he doesn't text you. You don't need him because there are plenty of other fish in the sea. Come on-let's go to a club." Nightclubs were our answer to every good or bad event that happened. So we hurriedly got ready so that we were dressed in our best heels and mini dresses with layers of makeup caked on. I opted for my usual all black club attire-black heels, black mini dress, and black smoky eyes-I felt hot.

A few other friends met us at the club after we pre-partied at our dorm since we would not be able to have access to the alcohol at the bar. We arrived at the club with a good buzz and we danced and danced. It was crowded at the club as usual. No one could stretch out their arms without hitting someone and receiving a dirty look. Nonetheless, as we felt the beat go through our feet and surge through our bodies we grew oblivious to our surroundings. I closed my eyes and danced as if I was touching heaven. It was like I was having a Shamanic experience in heels. Nothing mattered except this moment. At this moment I was letting go, letting go of my depression I went through in high school. I was letting go of my childhood and the nightmares that kept me anxious. I was letting go of being who everyone wanted me to be. I was letting go and I was almost free. Almost.

6

"Hey, over here!" I shouted and waved to Jimmy from across the street. It was a beautiful spring day in California and I was spending it with Jimmy AKA "Mr. I-Still-Like-You-Despite-The-Fact-That-You-Are-A-Prude." Seriously though, he ended up contacting me after a few weeks apologizing for his disappearing act. His reason was that he had never met a woman like me before and felt awkward since he did not know how to approach me from here on out. Whether or not I believed his excuse did not matter to me-I just wanted his attention and his luscious lips were an added bonus.

"Hey girl," he hugged me and smiled down at me, "Ready to go?"

"I'm ready but you gonna tell me where we're going yet?" I brushed a copper colored curl out of my eyes.

"Well, since you are a Pan African Studies minor and love to ramble on about the importance of activism and Black history, I thought you would love to check this out." He pointed towards what looked like a mini frat house. I was about to roll my eyes and ask what the hell was he thinking?? But as we walked closer I saw the sign on the door, "Black & Educated." I was shocked he remembered. I had told him when we first met that I had wanted to check out the B&E ever since I stepped foot on campus. It is HISTORICAL. I was almost hysterical.

The Black & E has been around for decades, ever since James Brown yelled, "I am Black and Proud!" My heart leaped-this was exciting. I had always dreamed about being part of a group of like-minded people who understood the importance of Black History and the American experience. I was gonna walk into the organization where the giants that came before me were a part of! I was gonna touch their vision. *Ok enough, be coo.* I told myself and calmed my stream of thoughts feeding off of the rush.

"We're allowed to go in?" I whispered feeling a ting of nervousness due to the fact that I was a newbie. "Yeah, I've never been here, but I was told they have an open door policy for students."

When we walked into the place I was met with beautiful art of famous Blacks and African Americans in history. There were my favorites: Langston Hughes, James Baldwin, Angela Davis, and the well-known Martin Luther King, Jr. staring back at me from the walls. Inside there was what looked like a huge living room with couches and chairs filled with Black students of every skin tone engaged in passionate discussion. Hmm-good crowd. Jimmy and I found a spot on the couch and settled in. I focused on what seemed to be the leader of the B & E, and fixed my eyes on her lips so I could read them. Apparently, the discussion was about how to improve the political consciousness of youth on campus and something else I could not yet pick up.

"Did anybody hear about what the School Board decided to do about this?" Asked the charismatic leader. She looked around the room and her eyes landed on Jimmy. "Oh hey, you're new here right?" She smiled at him warmly. "Yeah, she has always been interested in this kind of thing so I brought her here," he pointed at me. I began to smile at her and introduce myself but then I refrained. I refrained because she did not even glance in my direction. I tried again to say something and catch her eyes, but she did not smile warmly at me as she did at him. She rudely ignored me. I suddenly felt like an alien. An unwelcomed guest. There were no words for how taken back I felt. It was an avalanche of emotions. An ocean of thoughts. Jimmy did not seem to notice what had taken place. *Of course he didn't notice since he was a typical product of patriarchal society. Men.*

As they continued to chat I looked around the room. I scanned the faces carefully looking for a friendly face looking at me, but none could be found. I noticed their skin tones varied but the features were Black, African-American…like mine so what was the problem? Why was I invincible to them? Why didn't they see me? It could not be because I was deaf-my hair was down today covering my hearing aids and I voiced with Jimmy. That is when I realized they do not see me as one of them. I am not Black enough for them. I am invisible. My heart sunk deep into my stomach and drowned in my multiracial blood. There is no one-drop rule here. There is no "my people" here. I was nobody in a room full of Blacks and for the first time in my life I felt lonely with my people.

I thought of my Grandma and Papa-my father's parents. They were mostly Black. Papa's ancestors were from Ghana, Africa. They loved my sisters and I. They made me feel safe. Grandma never once shunned me. I was a part of them. We are from the same blood. So why had I been disowned by this *Black* organization? I bleed the same way they do and felt the same pains of living in White America. Perhaps that was not enough for them? Perhaps they saw my mother shinning through? If that be the reason then fuck it. My white mother and her parents ironically had more love for people than they did. My sadness turned to anger. I allowed the anger to build and it threatened to unleash the fury I buried all these years.

I got up and walked quickly back to my dorm with Jimmy at my heels. "Hold up!" He ran after me and grabbed my arm gently. "What's the hurry? Did I say something wrong?" "You really didn't notice anything that happened there??" I said incredulous although in the back of my mind I knew I should not have been surprised. Still I was hurt, angry, and as far as I was concerned he was part of the problem since he did not stick up for me. "No…I didn't…you mind filling me in?" He asked cautiously. And then in the middle of the night in front of my dorm I poured out my observations and interpretations as quickly as I could as if each word was poison and I had to get it out in order to live.

"Oh come on, you're overreacting," he exclaimed, "You really think you weren't acknowledged because they think you're not 'black enough'?" He rolled his eyes. I had missed what he said, so I asked him to repeat it. He did so and I curtly answered, "Yes." I said through gritted teeth and stormed through the doors to my room. Jimmy texted me attempting to apologize for being insensitive and hoped that we could agree to disagree and move on. I could not. I would not.

7

A few weeks had passed since the B & E incident. I had spoken with my father about the incident, which rarely happens, but I really wanted a father. So much that I was willing to ignore the bad dreams and memories just to fill a lie that blood is always thicker than water. Even if it meant drowning in that blood. So I had asked him his opinion about what ensued and he informed me that it was not my imagination that they had disregarded me. He had told me "They tend to accept dark skinned blacks since they were seen as "legitimate Blacks" "It's been like that since the 1970s I remember, but people in general are twisted, so do not let them get to you." He advised. *Court-Do not let them get to you. Humanity is twisted.* But how to "un-twist?" Anyway, I had begun repeating those droplets of wisdom since then. My parents were imperfect and wounded-they loved us to the best of their ability. I could always count on my Mum especially to provide comfort when life got too rough for my taste. Knowing those facts was enough for me to not be affected by mistakes they made.

I mulled over the conversation with my father as I walked to class enjoying the sun warming my face. If only it could warm my spirit. I felt as if my passion for fighting racism and for teaching Black History had been killed. It was I who let it die, but I wanted to place the blame elsewhere. Near my class I saw the B & E hosting a booth and handing out flyers. I felt anger rise up in me and then I took a breath. Without thinking, I strode towards the booth and reached out my hand for a flyer. The guy holding the flyers in his hand looked at me and grinned sympathetically at me as if I was a lost and confused little kid, "Uhh, sorry this is for Black students only." That was it-here I go. I had reached out my hand for the flyer but I knew I was not ready to forgive them, and give them a chance to explain the unknown wrong I felt they did to me. It was crazy I knew-they did not even know me or what I was angry about. Still I felt my hand remain extended then. I thought of saying these words that immediately came to mind;

> *I am no tragedy. I am Black and I hold that heritage close to my heart. I am White and Native American Indian and that is no tragedy either. My blood is pure whether or not I am one race or two. It is pure because the Spirit gave me breath.*

However, no longer able to hold back my rage I pulled back my hand and the next words spilled out of my mouth instead, "My father IS Black so FUCK YOU." He was stunned and shocked probably because this 'little light skinned girl' had some ovaries to say that to his face. I stormed away to class- I was late but I did not care because my anger had melted a tiny bit. No. That didn't happen. But I wished I had done that. So like that last patch of snow on the ground after a bitter winter, I knew it would take a long time before the anger within me vanished.

8

"Come on girl-let's go to a frat party," Pillar interrupted my thoughts as she walked into the living room of our dorm and handed me the flyer for the party. I groaned and set the flyer beside me on the couch. "I'm still hung over from the other night, how can you still be alive??" I asked her in disbelief. She laughed and looked down at me with her hand on her hip, "You know they say a cure for a hang over is a beer so lets get you one at the party." "And to answer your question-we live once right?" Pillar grinned and turned on JLo's *I'm Real*" as she danced off to get ready for the night. I cringed as I slowly got up from a peaceful siesta. *"Alright, time to suck it up and make the best of it,"* I muttered under my breath.

We arrived at the frat party with a few other friends and the minute we stepped into the house our senses were assaulted. The pungent smell of urine, men, puke, and alcohol was nauseating. I felt a wave swirl unpleasantly in my stomach and threaten to make its way to my mouth. "Ugh," I groaned and rubbed my nose as if I could rub away the smell. "Oh come on, you're exaggerating," Pillar rolled her eyes and pulled me towards the keg filled with cheap beer. This was a typical frat. Boys used their good looks to their advantage. One thing they did was seduce countless women (especially freshman) to their beds contaminated with bodily fluids. As I wondered silently how often they cleaned the filthy house Pillar shoved a red plastic cup filled with beer into my hand. I thanked her and sipped slowly. "I need air!" I yelled over the now loud music. Turning down the volume on my hearing aids did not even help at all. "Alright, I'll wait for you here!" Pillar yelled back then went back to downing her beer and struck up a conversation with some eye candy.

After elbowing my way through the crowd and slapping away the hands of testosterone driven males, I made it outside finally. I sat down on a once white lawn chair and breathed in the fresh air gratefully. I straightened out my sky blue "Venice Beach" shirt and leaned back. "Hey-you mind if I sit next to you?" I looked up and squinted in the dim lights and there he was- a tall, white, 'pretty boy' with brown hair and blue eyes. "Uhh…not at all," I smiled and gestured to the empty lawn chair next to me. "Thanks, it's getting pretty wild in there," He motioned towards the house. "Not surprised," I smiled and took a sip of my beer wondering why the hell he was talking to me when there were countless numbers of gorgeous white girls around.

"So you have a man?" He asked and smiled shyly. I looked at him a little confused and told him that I did not. He told me his name was Ben and that he wanted to take me out sometime. I turned him down gently as I did not feel a desire to date him or to give him a chance. "Oh come on, you know you're curious about me," Ben pushed and his shy smile disappeared. Like it was never there in the first place. Suddenly he was charming and alluring…almost deceptive. I pushed the word from my mind. *Giovanna, stop judging and overreacting just because he's white,* I silently reprimanded myself. "So what's it gonna be? It's ok to kinda like me you know?' He pressed and winked. I was silent for a while and then I forced myself to speak, "Alright, I'll go out with you." Sadness rolled in my stomach and I did not know why. *Perhaps because silenced once again a whisper that was trying to speak to me.* I ignored the soft voice within because that was what I was taught to do.

9

"Pillar!! You're so bad!" I exclaimed. "What?? I'm just speaking the facts," she giggled and flipped her hair over her shoulders. We were sitting in our favorite coffee/tea place near campus called Ebeez's and catching up with each other and gossiping. I had gone out on a date with Ben and things had become heated in a very good way. I was telling Pillar what I did with him….so far. She was giving me a hard time by suggesting all of these raunchy things I should try with him. We spent the rest of the afternoon gabbing like giddy high school girls, talking about our former crushes, and what we have done with men. We also talked about the different flavors of men we have been with and what our preferences were. As well as the other good and bad that comes with living. Children are resilient and are able to forgive a bit easier and heal a little better, but as adults it is a different story. So we enjoyed this moment, forgetting that we were already young adults and that our childhood was tarnished. It was a perfect moment, like we were 17 again as the song goes, and that we were unaware that the world had been cruel to us. We had tasted disappointment and felt shame, but a small part of us was still untouched and delicately intact. Me thinks that is a miracle.

10

Jimmy and I still talked but it was never the same as it was before. Ben was interesting for lack of better words. He was not my usual type. He was new, attentive…perhaps possessive but I could not let go. We had seen each other every week for the past few months and were growing attached with every moment. And I liked it because I was allowing myself to fall for the first time. The feeling was exhilarating; it was a rush I never felt before, like playing with fire despite the definite risk of getting burned. The night after I met him I had written down a few lines and did not know why I picked something so dark. Felt like a contrast to the fun I was having.

> "The rain it came
> I just laid my head down and prayed
> But no one came
> Maybe my tears will mimic the rain
> And wash out all this pain."

I walked over to Ben's apartment about 4 blocks away from me. He was having a kickback at his place as he usually does. As I was walking there I was trying to figure out where this was going. *Did he want a relationship or?* I was far from ready. When I walked into his apartment, I was met with a few familiar faces- his roommates and one of my interpreters whom I loved. Her style of interpreting was splendid. She was a beautiful fiery red head and did ASL justice so that the words and the meaning came alive. Plus her personality was warm and engaging. I made small talk with her and then strolled over to the bar area that was set up in the kitchen.

"Hey girl," Ben grinned and handed me a shot glass overflowing with tequila.

"Oh god," I murmured as I hesitantly took the glass. "We need to talk first," I blurted out and apologized to his friends for interrupting.

"Alright, no problem," Concern flashed across his face as he guided me to his room and shut the door.

"Well...what is this? We've been seeing each other for months now." I said slowly.

"We're dating right?"

"Yeah I guess we are, but I actually don't want a relationship yet." I scanned his face for any indication of disappointment or perhaps relief.

"No problem, we'll just keep dating. Cool?" He grinned again and his concern disappeared.

"Alright, well, that was easy." I laughed in relief. But I still could not shake the uneasiness that lingered in me and never let go.

That night I had 3 tequila shots and was still able to maintain. I flirted with anyone and everyone and made brilliant jokes. There was PDA happening all over the place in every corner, including between Ben and I. We had an intense sexual attraction to each other that I did not understand no matter how many times I tried to analyze it and dissect it for answers. One thing was clear though, Ben liked me more than I liked him and had told me drunkenly that I was his and he was not gonna let me go. He even proceeded to sing me a really corny song by the Backstreet Boys as he held me in his arms. I was flattered and giggled tipsily as I listened to his singing and then slept as I allowed the darkness to clothe me. Something in me surged like a hot rod of light in my stomach and I felt a sharp pain. I winced and blamed it on too much alcohol.

"Night falls
It just calls
And I try to give it my all
I close my ears
And listen with my heart
But sorrow still haunts
And there the light stalls
I close my eyes and try to feel
Someday I shall."

11

Summer. I always counted down the days until summer arrived even though boredom was sure to hit often since I was a broke college student who could not afford lavish traveling trips or my own car. Pillar and I always made the best of it by indulging in nightclubs, happy hour deals, and mini road trips home to Southern California. I was still seeing Ben casually, so we met up very often during the week. By summer I was aware of his flaws-perfectly aware and seeping into denial like quicksand. He at times made me feel like I was special and made only for him. Other times he made me feel stupid, small, and like I was a piece of shit. So much happened and so much was said that I could not retain all of the memories. I then grew tired of how he made me feel. I had no energy to ignore or to grasp tightly to the denial in hopes that his flaws would magically disappear. I had to confront him.

"Hey Ben, wanna meet up to go for a walk and talk?" I texted.

"Yeah sure, everything ok?" He replied back.

"I'll explain, meet me on the corner as usual."

I stood on the corner waiting for him anxiously. There was no telling how'd this go since I had tried to 'break up' with him before but always ended up caving in to his begging for me back. This time had to be different. I had to be stronger and let go of the fear that we may have something good that I will miss out on. It was nighttime and there was a slight breeze that made me shiver a bit even though it was summer. It made me think of the cold people feel when a ghost floats by. I pulled up my favorite low cut shirt in a futile attempt to block my chest from the cold. I crossed my arms in another attempt to keep warm when I felt Ben's presence. I turned around and smiled. We hugged tightly and then walked down the street. I rambled and rambled about my thoughts and my need for space from him. He listened carefully and did not say a word. "Well, what do you think about what I just said?"

"You just wanna be friends?" He asked for clarification.

"Yeah, I think it's best." I mumbled quickly.

"Ok, well then we can be friends." He smiled, "Come on, lets get something to eat."

I was stunned at how well he took everything. I smiled but somewhere in the back of my mind I was thinking, "He is taking this a little *too* well." I shook the thought from my mind and convinced myself that I was overanalyzing and that he was just being a good guy. A good friend, just like I always wanted. What was I so afraid of? I rolled my eyes at myself for being so fearful.

I was eating a delicious veggie burger with fries and he munching happily on his meat invested sandwich. "Well, this is nice huh? I'm glad we're friends now," I beamed. "Me too and hey Gia, I have a question."

"Yeah sure, sup?"

"When we were together would you have had sex with me?"

"Uhhh…" I almost choked on my fries at this random question.

"Honestly, no because I'd rather do it with someone special and someone I'm comfortable with. I am comfortable with you," I babbled quickly, "But I just rather wait until I know what I want so that I don't regret it. I will sometime but just not you." Oh boy, I was not making sense.

Ben laughed and looked away.

He didn't say anything and he had a funny look in his eyes that I had never seen before. It looked as if his soul had cowered away for a moment. It gave me the chills and made me feel uncomfortable. It was like there was something dark appearing behind his eyes not wanting to be found. *Stop it Sirena, you are really paranoid*, I reprimanded myself.

"Wanna go back to my place and drink-celebrate our new friendship?" He winked.

"Ohh, good idea," I felt giddy and cool. I would now have a heterosexual guy friend and perhaps I'd be able to get advice about men from him. I strolled happily back to his place dragging along my friendship fantasies.

"To us." We clinked our shot glasses together and laughed. Damn, this felt nice. Maybe I was wrong about him and his destructive flaws? Maybe I should give him a second chance? *NO, he was manipulative and made me feel small. We are friends now and that is much healthier. Damn it, I need another shot to drown this mounting paranoia. What if I'm going crazy? They say the 20s are delicate periods and psychotic breaks are common.*

"I need another shot!" I exclaimed loudly. This was my third...or fifth? I could not remember-everything was foggy. I just remembered feeling safe and cozy there on the couch with Ben. We laughed and talked about random things. "Damn, how many shots have you had?" I asked him. "Just 2." I stopped smiling and had no idea why. Ben was well known for his high tolerance for alcohol. He usually drank 8 shots to feel just a slight buzz. It took him way more than that to get drunk. He seemed to have noticed the disappearing act of my smile because he reassured me that everything was ok, "Don't worry, I will catch up with you, I just need to go slow cause I drank a lot the other night." Something in me screamed, *"Lie, lie." What the fuck was wrong with me?* I was angry at myself for constantly being so judgmental and suspicious. After all he was the one who a long time ago had lectured me about dating "bad guys" in the past, so he couldn't be that bad, I reasoned. "Come on, have fun, you deserve it," He handed me another shot of tequila. I drowned it as if it was the answer to everything. I started to fade quickly. I was floating and did not want the feeling to end. I felt myself being guided to his room. It was so quiet and dark. His roomies were not home. For some unknown reason I looked back at the kitchen table and noticed the bottle of tequila was not even half empty and he was still sober. *I am not sober,* I giggled. Then all my senses went silent.

When I came to I was on my back in his bed. He was lying beside me and I felt him touch my arm. I felt confused and then I blacked out again. A couple more times the scenario repeated. I began panicking when I realized this is what people call "blacking out." I had no control-my worst fear. Then out of nowhere I felt a surge of pain rip the flesh between my thighs. I whimpered and realized my clothes were not on my body anymore. It was so cold where I lay and my body was paralyzed with alcohol. I opened my heavy eyes and saw him hovering over me. The pain was unbearable and my eyelids betrayed me. They closed as the pain tore through again and I could not open them again until the dawn crept slowly into the room.

12

I slept walked on through the days. It was as though I had left my body and was watching myself live my pathetic life on earth below. Ben had apologized countless times and had cleverly convinced me that he was truly sorry and had not meant to do what was done. Still numb and in denial of all that had taken place I forced myself to believe him. I had to believe his lies-it was the only way I could survive the scene that was seared onto my soul like a tattoo you futilely wish you could erase. My friends were worried, they were angry with him. Some did not believe my story and that hurt the most. Some were angry with me and did not understand my need to get back with him. Some thought because I was "too friendly," and that I brought it on myself. Pillar was the only one who saw through me. She somehow helped me through the shock and then I pulled my mask of "everything is ok" tightly over my face and it seemed to work. Everyone eventually thought I was fine and dandy. I was not a victim I told myself every second until I lived it. A few weeks later he had lied to everyone and claimed he never did anything to me that night. I felt like someone had taken a knife and jammed it into my belly button and split it open until it hit my stomach. Still I smiled. I smiled until I felt nothing. After all, ghosts cannot feel. At least I wished they couldn't, so I wrote:

"I'm alive
Still I crave the grave
I love life sometimes
And appreciate what you gave."

13

"Whoohooo!!" Pillar yelled as she ran over to me. "Can you believe we graduated??" She cried excitedly. "I know huh? 5 years and here we are!" I hugged her and the tears spilled over and I felt as if they'd never stop. She hugged me back tightly and began to sob with me. I would miss her presence and our spontaneous outings. She had been my *rock* through college and I hoped I had been hers too. "Keep in touch alright?" I smiled through my tears. We held hands and then walked away to our waiting families. I pondered if our promises to keep in touch were empty. "Giovanna Black!!" I recognized the sound of my name and glanced around to identify where it was coming from. In the distance near one of the palm trees I saw him. Jimmy walked over to where I was standing with my family in my navy blue cap and gown. His familiar smile gave my heart little butterflies and I could not help but break out into a cheesy grin. "Hey Jimmy, been too long," We hugged and exchanged a few meaningless words before reuniting with our families. I will always wonder what could have been with him, but I know that it was not meant to be for whatever reason. Shoulda been. Coulda been. Tomatoe. To-mah-to. I sighed and walked away. The sky was blue with no cloud in sight. I would be ok eventually. I could feel sweat burning my armpits and my throat closing up. I could not breathe. It was a new 'phenomenon' that had started happening during my college years. At the time I couldn't pinpoint or fathom the cause of this change in my body. I could not make it stop. I had no control. My body betrayed me. And the feeling that everything would be ok died right then and there. I buried the feeling under piles of ash until it stunk like decay throughout my entire being.

14

"Mom!! Look!" I screeched as I ran into the kitchen. "Giovanna, take a breath," she said covering her ears and putting down the knife she was using to chop vegetables for dinner. I handed her the letter that had arrived in the mail this morning. "What??" She read it fast and looked up at me. "Congrats!! That is so exciting!! Did you tell your father?"

My parents were now divorced, so I went between two different houses to spend time with each of my parents. It was not too bad since I had been away from home for so long. I could not speak for my sisters though. Perhaps they felt differently, I would never know. All I knew was that I got an acceptance letter to one of the top universities in New York City for graduate school. I picked up my phone to text my father the good news-he'd be proud too like my mother was. I swore I would never leave California-it was my home. Los Angeles especially had molded and shaped me. From the Dickies wearing days, cholo crushes, to the present moment as a more mature, resilient adult. It was my heart. But things change and people change as well. The tide was moving and I had to go with it, there was no swimming backwards or else I'd just drown. I didn't want to drown anymore.

The night before I was to fly out to New York City I reminisced a bit. I took in the dry cool air of the California night. I took in the comforting palm trees lined up along the street. It was bittersweet leaving, and as my thoughts flowed the bitter tasted stronger. I thought of that guy I dated. Then I thought of them in elementary school grabbing my small breasts that had begun to form and anger rose. I remembered myself lying on the floor confused when I was 3. Tears welled up in my eyes and spilled over my pillow. I lay there drenched in liquid prayers and remembered I had cut myself with a needle during High School. I'd vow to never do it again. But he triggered so much shit and HS memories made me sick to my stomach. So a few days ago I found a needle in my room and burned it with fire from my lighter. I slowly began to drag cuts into my skin again. I was careful. I picked places that would not see daylight. At times I hoped I'd bleed out and never wake up again. Then I'd feel guilty for thinking such awful thoughts, so I would cry when the sun hit my eyes reminding me that I was still alive.

15

New York City. Home. It *actually* felt like home. The way the immense amount of diversity in people and such merged together to form something that words could not describe. It was like each step outside was urging me to live my life to the fullest. There was no time to die or to think about dying-the only option was to live. That was New York City to me. No way I could be invincible to the intense energy that was begging to be breathed in. With each step I took I felt like I was in a dream-like state of mind. Even the classes in graduate school were pure bliss. Classmates poured out their thoughts and opinions regarding theories and philosophies while professors polished our minds to prepare for what lay ahead for us in the "real world." Whatever the "real world" really means.

I remember my older sister and I, when we were kids, asking our Mum if we could live in NYC together. I do not recall where we got the idea of living in NYC, but it is what it is. And it is quite strange that I ended up in NYC after all this time vowing to stay in CA. And the even funnier thing was that my older sis had lived in NY for a few years for college. Isn't it funny how things turn out? Is our life already mapped out for us? Kind of like Alice in Wonderland when she tries to find her way back home, but it was as if the universe pushed her along the path she was meant to go.

As I left class I waved bye to my two interpreters and walked toward St. Marks Ave in the numbing winter. I could not type to my friends that I had arrived at the bar we agreed to meet at-my hands were paralyzed from the cold. I thrust my hands in the pockets of my new Eco-Friendly coat I wore proudly and a bit self-righteously. *Damn it.* I muttered to myself. *I can't believe I forgot my fucking gloves.* "Boo!!" Kent jumped out at me then laughed and laughed at my reaction. According to him I looked like I had come face to face with my worst nightmare: Sarah Palin. I hit Kent on the arm and then we walked into the bar together. *Thank goodness we were out of the cold.*

We took our coats off and squeezed between the crowds. We surprisingly found seats at the bar and I put my coat on a 3rd chair for when Raquel arrived. While Kent ordered his usual vodka I scanned the crowd. It has always been a habit of mine to observe which characters were in play and where they seemed to be in their chapter of this life. Act 1? Act III? I then thought of the movie, Crash, and the quote in the beginning, "Sometimes we miss that touch so much we crash into each other just to feel something." I wondered who here was crashing, and who wasn't. Satisfied with my scan of the room I turned back to face the bar and ordered a Tequila Sunrise. They didn't have White Russian. *Pfft.*

"You see anyone you like??" Asked Kent over the loud music, conversation, and clinking of glasses. He ran a hand through his blonde faux Mohawk. "Not really! What about you?" I shouted back signing lazily. Kent paused and looked around the room casually. "Not my type-oh wait." "Look over there." He signed and grinned. As smoothly as possible I pretended to check out the tacky art work on the bar wall, then I glanced over to where Kent had motioned. There stood this very "Brooklyn" looking guy. The Brooklyn before the Hipsters took over under the category of gentrificators. He had a nice black coat on with a NY cap, nice jeans and shoes. His eyes were kind and his stance was confident and sexy. I could not guess his nationality. *Perhaps Puerto Rican, but I can't assume.*

"Ohhhh I hope he's straight." I crooned to Kent. "He definitely is you idiot-go for it," he nudged me gently. "No! I don't want to embarrass myself," I whispered firmly and sipped my drink as coolly as possible. Kent rolled his eyes and made conversation with a gorgeous "Bear" sitting next to him. Someone tapped me on my shoulder. I turned around and began to smile flirtatiously. "Oh! Raquel…I thought…never mind," I chuckled sheepishly. Rae laughed and gave Kent and me a hug. "I think I failed my fucking midterm. Ughh," she complained as she settled into her chair and took off her coat. "I am so sick of grad school. How was your test?" She asked me. "It was awful, but I think I probably got a B-but whatever. I'm just gonna enjoy my night."

We toasted and made small talk about how long we wanted to stay at the bar. We then started joking and making fun of various people. We laughed and laughed as we usually do while Kent pretended that he did not know us to avoid the possibility of us turning away potential 'suitors' for himself. Rae made another wisecrack and I doubled over in laughter, slapping my thigh and then I looked up in mid-laughter and came face to face with "The-Cute-And-Possibly-Puerto-Rican-Brooklyn-guy." I was so embarrassed. I had been laughing inhibited and hadn't bothered to cover my mouth as I usually do to cover my flaring nostrils, visible tonsils (exaggeration), and my now alcohol laden breath.

"Brooklyn Guy" smiled and asked me what my name was. *Thank goodness I can read his lips so far.* I thought. I told him my name and he said his name was Marvin. He had a sweet smile and long eyelashes that made him look innocent although it was plain to see that he had lived a rough life. *Ah, there was something behind his eyes.* We made small chit-chat and then he left me with his text number. I texted him the next day and about a week later we agreed to meet up for lunch.

16

"Ughh! I don't know what to freakin' wear!" I sighed in utter frustration and plopped on my dorm bed. "Giovanna, relax! This looks good on you so just wear this," Kent reassured me and held up my favorite black, tight plunging V-neck shirt and black heeled Steve Madden boots. A little flutter of relief and then excitement stirred up in me. "I think that will work," I smiled and took the shirt and boots from him and threw them on with my dark blue jeans that bring out the curves in my thighs. "Yes, we both know it will look good because you ALREADY tried it on before!" Kent rolled his eyes. I smiled sweetly at him mockingly. *How he put up with my craziness I will never know.*

"Ok shoo, shoo. Have fun, kiss him, fuck and whatever else you need to do," Kent said pushing me out of my room and into the hall. I laughed. His bluntness never ceased to amuse me. It was refreshing to encounter so much honesty in a world of immense fiction and mind games. We hugged bye and parted ways on Bleeker Avenue. As I walked to the train to meet Marvin for lunch I felt a mixture of nervousness at the unknown, but happiness that my outfit looked so good. I couldn't wait to show off. I strutted down the train station stairs.

17

I arrived just in time to see Marvin walking into the restaurant as well. Something about him made me feel comfortable-at home. He saw me looking at him and smiled charmingly. We hugged briefly and awkwardly and then allowed the waiter to show us to our table. We sat down across from each other and nervously sipped the ice-cold tap water that was probably reaming with pollutants and chloride. "You're very beautiful."

"Thanks," I giggled like a 17 year old, "So how has your day been?"

"It's been pretty long 'cause of work ya know? But it is what it is. I work for a lawyer but trying to work my way up."

"Ah, so you're in the con business?" I smirked. *That was lame.* I thought to myself. *And where the fuck is the waiter? I wanna order now. This is awkward.*

Laughing, Marvin looked at me and said, "I can see you are a tough one,and no I am not in the "con" business just because I work for a lawyer. So tell me what you do?"

I smiled, "I know, I was just messing. So anyway, I am student here-grad student in Social Work. I just moved out here from California so still getting used to this weather." I motioned wryly out the booth window covered in frost.

"Ah-a California girl. LA?"

"Yeah, Los Angeles," I said nodding proudly.

"The hood I see. You got a little gangster in you?" He hit my arm playfully.

"Pfft, not all of Los Angeles is that way. But yes, I did grow up around that a bit 'cause of my older sister and her friends. I did see the glamour in it. False glamour." I added.

LA in the 90's was no joke but it was a part of me. I grew, I learned, and I lived dipping my toes into the culture but never embracing it 100%. All my life it felt like every time I tried to jump into something "risky," a hand or hands were holding me back. They would only let me get my feet wet, like an overprotective parent at their child's first swim lesson. Some of the best and worse years of my life were dished out in my overall Dickies and bandanas tied up 2Pac style. A lot of embarrassment for me to look back on it but still I had no regrets. It made me strong, proud, and gave me an identity when I had none.

"I grew up in the Bronx, and uhh… I actually was trouble. It was tough." He chuckled sadly. *He still trouble.* Something told me. "But anyway, I have come a long way from all of that bullshit. I want to be a better example for my cousins and my son-" He looked at me obviously watching my reaction to the last words out of his mouth. "Oh, a son?" I tried hard to sound "neutral" and "nonchalant" but I am pretty sure it showed I was trying too hard and that a million questions were swimming through my head. He told me the story. I listened. I saw the good within the fact and the fiction. And I hung on.

The next day I went with Rae to a bar on 52nd street. We talked about our upcoming papers we had to type and the latest guys we liked but could not have. "Let's go to the Couch Surf event-it's happening now!!" Rae exclaimed showing me a text she received from Alla a fellow couch surfer. "Good idea! We'll meet more interesting international people." We paid for our drinks and ran to the A train downtown. On the train we always ended up cracking up at the things we would see and hear-NYC never fails to provide some kind of entertainment each step of the way. We got off at our stop and walked into the bar. The event was upstairs, so we walked up the wooden stairs to the 2nd floor. There in the dim room with a lighted bar were handfuls of beautiful people from every nationality it seemed, and us boring Americans.

"Hey Alla," we hugged and said hello to her entourage. Alla was a beautiful blonde with model-like features that would make any woman want to strangle her or perhaps fuck her. Alla's "entourage" as I called them were just as equally beautiful. The group consisted of 2 women from Sweden, and an American guy who had a pet tiger as he later showed us a picture. Last but not least was a tall, lanky man from France, who was just visiting NYC (couch surfing). "Nice to meet you all," Rae and I said as All introduced us to each one. No way I could remember or comprehend all of their names. There was just too much happening for Rae and I to keep up lip reading. As we all became more comfy with each other's accents, and personality they wanted to learn a few signs so we obliged.

"Be right back, I'm gonna get another beer," I SimCommed to Rae. I walked over in my Steve Madden boots to the bar, feeling highly confident. The French guy followed me and that boosted my ego even more. "Let me get that," he said paying for my drink. "Aww thanks," I giggled and then prayed I could continue understanding what he says. "So are you single," he smiled a bit shyly. "Umm…I'm sorry, can you say that again?" Shit. I could not understand what he said. After about 2 hours of lip reading, my brain usually shuts down exhausted. French guy got out a piece of paper from his pocket and borrowed a pen from the bar. He wrote down; *Are you single*? "Oh, yes I am. Are you?" I smiled. French guy nodded. Then all of a sudden I saw Rae's latest hook up walk into the bar. *She will be so happy he's here,* I thought to myself.

After a quite a bit of writing back and forth with the French guy, I got bored and excused myself. I walked through the crowd and spotted Rae's hook up again….there were two of him! He has a twin! I scurried over to Rae and told her that Mr. Hookup has a twin and pointed in his direction. Rae looked at me and slowly blinked, "That's a mirror." I looked again and yep; there was indeed a mirror right next to the bar. I was so embarrassed, and then we of course burst out laughing really hard. Laughter- tis good for the soul just like they say.

18

When night covers the sky the world takes note and becomes quieter. Well at least that is how it is supposed to be. Nowadays no one pays attention anymore. It is like the galaxies are a distant memory. Invisible. Does anyone even remember to see the stars anymore? It is like they no longer exist. Laying so close to the window in my graduate dorm right in the pulse of Manhattan made it hard to take on the quietness. Every night I was fully aware that this city doesn't sleep and that a million people who are lonely and empty roam the city like ghosts looking for their next fix in whatever way, shape or form it comes in. It is so easy to get used to the noise to the point where we are afraid of the silence. We wish there were a million electric lights dotting the dark instead of soft glimmers of stars and a distant moon trying to whisper to us something we need. We need something that cannot be found in this kind of life yet we stifle out the whispers. I turned over in my bed and looked up to my beige ceiling. *God, it's so lonely here. I wonder if anyone else feels the same?* Tears fell down my face and I became angry. Angry I could not control the liquid from my eyes running over my cheeks. I could not see my need. What I needed. So instead I got out of bed and turned on my phone. *Yes!* Marvin had texted me and asked me to meet up with him in an hour. I jumped in the shower and threw on my clothes, grabbed my purse and Metro card and slammed the door. I walked into the artificially lit night.

19

"Wow, this is good!" I said eating the coconut ice cream that Marvin had bought over to my dorm. He laughed, "I told you. It was always my favorite since I was a little hoodlum." Since my roommate was gone for the weekend, we had my room to ourselves and we sure made the best of it. He never healed me fully. In fact he opened up a couple of old wounds, but still he made me feel like I was as beautiful as Alicia Keys or Beyonce. Like I was the 'only girl in the world' as the song goes. I know it sounds corny, but there is no better way to describe it. Marvin was complicated. Angry. Intelligent. Yet I let him con his way into my heart hoping that he'd change for the better. I saw his potential.

"You mentioned starting your own gang when you were 13, what's up with that?" I asked. Marvin laughed, "Well, my hood wasn't exactly the best. I mean you had to you know protect yourself or else you were a target. So I just went for it… and…and it was pretty good for a while…" He paused. He proceeded to tell me horror stories about fights he endured and times he barely made it alive. He told me of his cousin who was murdered and how he was worried about his family. I listened intently and stroked his arm comfortingly. I had a feeling at the time that although he was being honest, he was leaving out huge chunks of information. When he was done with his storytelling he looked me in the eye, "That didn't scare you did it?"

"What? Definitely not. I grew up in Southern CA during the 90's with all that gang violence happening. Always looking over our shoulder if we wore red or a bandana for style, so that doesn't faze me." I smiled. He stood up and pulled me to my feet. *Aww he's probably gonna hug me and tell me that he appreciates me listening so genuinely, and then we're gonna get it on baby.* Instead he looked me again in my eyes with his famous intense gaze and said, "So if someone wanted to hurt me I would just take this knife," and I watched in stunned silence as he removed a small knife from his pocket I never even knew was there. And then he pointed it between my thighs with his finger. He continued, "All I have to do is slice him from here to here," and he traced his knife lightly from between my thighs to below my rib cage.

"Oh." I whispered.

"The reason for that is you will lose just as much blood as you would cutting the neck." He explained with an eerie calm. As if he did not notice my uncomfortable silence he continued explaining the best way to bleed someone out. My jaw clenched shut and my muscles tensed to the point where I felt paralyzed. He then hovered over me and I struggled and struggled. Thoughts sliced my mind, *I cannot be a victim again. I won't survive if I am. I'll pretend it didn't happen. Yeah, I'll pretend like I have always done.* I closed my eyes and tried to breathe, but something in me died again. The ironic part was that I was not haunting anyone-I was the haunted.

"So then you know how it goes
Softly it drops like snow
Sweet tasting like the rose
Humble I lay among this prose
Words dance around my body and sink into my soul
I close my eyes and smile
'Cause nobody knows
I'm just drowning and don't know care where I go."

20

Time drags on when you're just floating through life lifeless. A year that felt like five long ones had passed. A year filled with much happiness and grief equal in measure. The expenses of being in a city that robs pockets had taken a toll. I had gained and lost so much in soul and mind. I grew into a better person because of it all, but the student loans that mounted had begun to stunt my growth. So I packed my bags and left NYC. I knew I would cry every day and night for those I left behind. And I did. Kent and Rae had been my sanity when I broke up with Marvin a couple months ago. They had been my joy when sadness seeped in. And they were my reality check when I got lost in my twisted bundle of thoughts. Yeah, I packed my bags and realized I was what people call "dragging around baggage." When all of the stuff you go through weighs you down, because you won't or don't know how to unpack and let go of what is dead weight. The key they say is to just let it go because you don't need it no more. Sigh…I closed my eyes on the plane to LAX and silently mulled over and over in my head. I drifted off to sleep and didn't realize I should have taken my gut's voice of wisdom to heart. But I just couldn't feel.

21

California. Home. Heart. And memories. They come and go like the seasons as they say. The hard thing to accept is that sometimes when it is summer, the heart and soul are still living in a winter. I felt myself growing colder and colder. I remained numb and I masked it well. Too well. I walked out into Mum's living room where she was putting up pictures in her new apartment. "Hey Mum, Wilson just texted me and asked if we can hang out tonight so I'm gonna take up his offer on that." I dreaded my mother's response. I could imagine it in my head, *"What??" "Who??" "Giovanna, isn't that the guy you liked for a long time but he seemed to be playing games?" "What are you **really** looking for?"* My mother had a knack for reaching deeper and deeper into why you chose to do something until you find yourself either breaking down into tears and confessing all or doing the opposite-struggling to keep a poker face. Needless to say, I was not in the mood for soul searching. I just wanted to see Wilson and fuck…talk…and forget that I was NOT in NYC.

Mum put down the picture of a beautiful lotus thriving and laying in the sun among the muddy waters. I looked at the muddy waters. *'Still waters run deep with you,' someone once told me.* She turned to look at me and rolled her eyes. "What?" She exclaimed, just as I had predicted, "What you guys gonna do??" "Uhhh…hang out. Catch up." I replied as if the answer was obvious. "Ok…well…just let me know where you are and page me if anything comes up." She said a bit disapproving with one hand on her hip. She had that look that said, "I wish you had made a better choice but since you are old enough I cannot tell you what to do so just be careful." I smiled with amusement that this will always be who she is. Despite her tendencies she is my mother and I love her for that.

Wilson. Oh boy, how to describe him? He had eyes that look like they hold secrets and mysteries that captivated multitudes of women. He was originally from El Salvador and his presence and physical appearance showed it. It seeped through his every pore in the way he talked, walked, dressed, and smiled. He was perfection to me at that time. We had known each other for 5 years and I could have fallen in love with him, but I refrained knowing I did not want a relationship at the time with anyone. Still, I sometimes think I did fall for him…accidently. Possible to accidently fall in love? Who knows? I stood on the corner of my mother's block waiting for Wilson to pick me up for dinner and then a show. I glanced nervously at my pager waiting for the, "I'm here," text. It had been about an year since I'd last seen him.

About 5 minutes later my phone vibrated. My heart leaped and I began to sweat a bit from anxiety. *I'm here, I see you.* I looked around and lo and behold there he was standing outside of his blue mustang looking like a salvador with the sun shining behind his back. *Could he save me?* I walked towards him and tried my best to walk sexy and appear confident. I was concentrating so hard on trying to make my legs appear long and graceful that I did not see the huge rock in front of me. I tripped. But I broke my fall just in time before I really humiliated myself. Shit-he saw the whole thing. Wilson just smiled and calmly asked if I was ok. I tittered like a 13 year old, "Oh, I'm fine. So great to see you again!" and we hugged. He opened the car door for me and off we went to dinner. We chatted like no time had passed and it really felt comfortable and familiar to me. He was the 2nd guy I had sex with back in my undergrad college years after *the* guy…Ben. It was my first healthy, mutual and 100% consensual sexual relationship with no strings attached. Truth be told, he was the one who noticed I was inexperienced and had asked about my first time: I shrugged it off but he called my first time "date rape." That was the first time anyone had really called it what it was and did not say it was my fault. And for that I could not help but love…like him. He was there and he saw me.

"Do you have to go to DC?" Wilson asked me as we were laying in some cheap hotel before he dropped me off at home. I had been accepted to a Deaf University in DC where

I planned to finish my Master's degree. This would be the last time we saw each other. I looked at him and did a double take at the randomness of his words. He was not the kinda guy to say or do "mushy" "romantic" stuff. I laughed a bit and hesitantly replied, "Yeah, I do." I did not know his intent in asking me that; to charm me, make me feel good, or was he seriously asking me that question? I will never know. I laid my head back down on his bare chest and continued running my fingers over his toned, light mocha colored skin. He sighed a bit. I could never read him well. He remained a mystery to me still after more than five years. "Alright, I better get back home."

Wilson drove me home and when I got out of the car I blurted out, "I'll miss you." He smiled at me and for the life of me I could NOT read his smile. I immediately became embarrassed for confessing that I will miss him. I sounded so…needy…pathetic…and wimpy. Eww. I waved sheepishly and walked up the stairs to my Mum's apartment. We sisters called it the Tree house because it was surrounded by huge, beautiful, protective trees. *I wonder if there are tree spirits. How nice would that be.* I looked in my Mum's room where she was sleeping peacefully and grabbed my PJs and changed. I then settled into my temporary room and mulled over the night's events for a bit. Time to let him go. I did not know that I would never see him again after that night. If a fortune teller had come up to me and told me that fact-I would have cried my eyes out that night until I was so exhausted that I had no choice but to welcome sleep.

22

Summer comes again. Funny how time just ticks on and on. California isn't really different in the summer except for the energy. It's lighter and more positive among us native Californians. My mother, my sisters and me took a road trip from home all the way to Indiana to visit some of my mother's family first before they dropped me off at Gallaudet.

Indiana…oh boy…how to describe such a backwards state. The irony of it all is that in the midst of the red necks, racist country people, and Confederate flags people forget that the very word 'Indiana' means, "Land of the Indians." It is not the racists land. They are living on stolen land. The First Nation people were almost wiped out completely when Europeans came to America and took over. Year after year they mascaraed them and no one could or would stop them. I imagine that beneath the ground six feet under contain the blood, bones, and ghosts of the natives that were murdered. They are slowly awakening and waiting for the day of revenge. A spiritual vendetta. I have also imagined that their spirits are among us and are guiding justice in their own ways. That brings me some comfort that somewhere there is justice being dished out for those who have been violated. But it is always short-lived when a white man in a pickup truck waves a Confederate flag at me. Taunting me. If I were a ghost I'd pop up in his truck and shred his flag to pieces and haunt him in his dreams every night. I wondered if I'd ever feel safe in this world while I was still alive? Perhaps I'd be better off as a ghost sleeping peacefully in the arms of my ancestors and the Spirit…universe?

"Bye Gramps!" I gave him a hug then stepped away to let my sisters and Mum say their goodbyes as well. I observed him as I waited to hit the road again to DC. He was 96 years old and his mind was still running. My mother got her integrity from him-he was a thinker. And he was loyal to his wife even after she died…no men like that left in this world. *I will miss him*. I tried to swallow the lump that had formed in my throat. As the good people from his generation died such as Coretta Scott King, etc. I felt more and more alone and *terrified* of the world. I felt like a 3-year-old child whose parents woke up one morning and left without a word or any warning. Living on Earth was akin to living in an orphanage sometimes.

We walked to the Shoe that was amazingly still running after all these years and turned to wave bye one last time to Gramps. He stood in the doorway with his polished wooden cane and smiled. His smile was one of joy and sadness mixed together. It was always bitter sweetness. I buckled up and glanced at my mother and tried to read her face. I saw a twinge of the same joy and sadness. My mother was a warrior. She was fierce. She survived my father and other stuff. Still I could see her eyes fade off as if she was remembering a better time. I glanced at my sisters and could not read them. We are so much alike in the way we deal with emotions and anxiety…we don't deal. I looked away.

23

1865-the year the university I was now attending was founded. This made me think long and hard about those who came before me and what their experience was like; double oppression of racism and audism. Shit-imagine me as a woman during that time! Triple oppression even now! Luckily I was born a fighter so somewhere within all of the deadness and sorrow I was still trying to box my way to light. Unlike the great Muhammad Ali I did not won yet.

I was walking down H Street so I could clear my mind of its cluttered thoughts and get some Chai tea at my favorite Somalia café. I arrived at the café and mulled over my thoughts as I watched successful Black people dressed sharply walk past me outside. I smiled a bit and wondered if I'd ever teach Black studies like I always wanted to do when I was finished with grad school. Then my thoughts switched to the fact that I survived a traumatizing dating experience with a woman who was textbook borderline.

I also survived a woman who made me love my body again, as well as sex just for its pleasure and not solely for the escape it provides. Yet, I was scarred by her because of her faults. She was my first true romantic relationship, and the first person I gave my heart to and professed my love for. We were intense together in a sweet and bitter way. But she manipulated well and made me think I was crazy. My gut screamed every time I was with her that she was never quite honest with me and her doings with her toxic roommate. It killed each time and it killed again when she wanted to live with that sicko as a roommate again. Why? Why I stayed with her time and again and ignored my voice screaming to leave? But it made me stronger. In fact, I have her jersey number tattooed on me to remind me of the time she healed me physically and taught me how to make love. But ironically because of her I was more determined not to fall in love again.

I finished the last drop of my Chai tea latte and walked back to my dorm. I did not know what I would do next and where I would be. I thought of death again because I did not see anything hopeful in the future. I did not know if I'd ever see my close friends again that I had lived with, cried with, and laughed with nearly everyday. I thought of the grave because I could not think of the births to come. Who'd see me and hear me? That night we all partied together one last time before we all went off after we graduated. I drank and glued on a fake smile. I waved bye and gave hugs and acted as if I was strong enough to withstand my heart breaking again as the loneliness solidified like a headstone.

That night I fantasized that I landed in California and went straight to the hotel I booked for one night. I had lied and told my family and friends that I would be landing in California in two days. I then showered, and changed into my favorite pajamas with a shirt that said, "Los Angeles," that I had gotten from my older sister. It had a chola with the classic dark lip stick and gelled up hair giving the beloved "LA" sign. I laid out my will and the letters for all the people I loved. The letters were marked with my gratefulness for them and my wishes for them to go on to live fulfilled and happy lives and then I'd rest happily. I fought back tears as I placed the letters made out to; Mum, Dad, my two sisters, and my friends; Pillar, Kiwi, Jasmine, Raquel (Rae) and Kent, etc. etc. etc. *Ok I'm ready.* I tried to convince myself to stop the drops of hot tears and smile because finally the constant pain, anxiety, and nightmares would end. But ironically the more I smiled the more I cried and became sadder. Faking happiness can have that effect.

I opened the bottle of vodka and the sleeping pills I got from the store yesterday. I downed them all and sobbed all the way through. I would dearly miss everyone. I hoped they would not be too sad and would not mourn for me too long. The guilt of causing that would be unbearable. *Hopefully they understand this is the best decision I had to make for myself.* I whimpered and then smiled a bit as I welcomed what I thought was death. *I'm ok now.* I smiled again and this time it was not fake.

24

The sun...the light hit me. I opened my eyes and my heart fell. I had fallen asleep while daydreaming about my death...I was not dead...Damn it. No way this was heaven or whatever you wanna call it as I glanced fervently around my bedroom. I cussed as loudly as possible. I did not give a shit that someone could have heard me. Because I just could *not* fathom how I still had breath left in me. How the fuck was I alive after downing a whole bottle of vodka and a bottle of sleeping pills? Oh right-it was just a daydream. I felt nauseous. Fucking frustrated. I should be feeling happy and crying tears of joy that I was alive, but no I was fucking pissed my body was moving and functioning. And I was angry at God, the Source. Where is He/She in all of this?

I looked out the window of my bedroom and contemplated jumping out. Then I looked at my phone and saw the messages from everyone, including Kent who was anticipating meeting up with me tomorrow in DC. A small ting of guilt creeped up in me, but I shook it off. *I'll try this suicide thing another time,* I muttered. I searched through my makeup bag and found my handy pocket knife and took my jeans off. I then sat on the edge of my bed and spread my legs. I then glided the blade against my inner thighs-carefully measuring how far I could go without the cuts peeking through shorts or skirts. I then pressed harder until the blood gushed out a little bit more. I lingered at the blood that pooled outside of the cut into a tiny puddle. *'I'm alive,'* I weeped and hung my head. I lay carefully back against the bed and let the blood dry so it could form a scab. I stared at the white ceiling feeling numb.

The sun mocked me for the next few months with it's brightness and the moon made me wish it would disappear so it'd be pitch black. I tried my best to hide my sadness and succeeded most of the time. No one knew or seemed to suspect I was swimming in deep darkness and sorrow. No one saw the old and new scars across the skin on my left buttocks and on my inner thighs. No one saw me cringe when a new scab dried and became stuck to my jeans. No one knew I secretly changed the Band-Aids when I cut a bit too deep. *The first cut is the deepest the song says-I wonder how he thought of that title. Wait a minute maybe all of these depressing thoughts of suicide are my spirit's way of telling me I need to go to California to kill the old me metaphorically so I can be renewed like the Phoenix. No that's stupid.* I pushed the theory from my mind.

25

Days go by like an old freight train. They keep going and going and you cannot stop it with your hands or a word. Hope has been a funny thing with me, it never lets me go no matter how much I shove it away. I think it was a TV show character that said, "Hope is funny, you cling to it and it clings back." After about 2 years I was back in New York City; the city that was part of my one time healing and gave me a place to call home. A place to grow and live in heaven for about a year. A very memorable year. I had gotten a job at a school because of some connections from college and was sort of happy. Also, Kent and I were roommates in a shady part of Brooklyn. By shady I mean that we had neighbors who punched holes in the walls during arguments with each other, constant drunk parties with toddlers in tow, and a break-in the 1st month I moved in with Kent. I cannot tell you the number of times I thought of calling Child Protective Services on them…and did one time. But the system failed of course. Anyway, the 'hood had some good things though… like the authentic Italian pizza place on the corner. Yeah, that was the only positive about it. Later on even that turned sour when the owner insulted me when we tried to order delivery through VRS. Pfft. Ignorant folks are not only in the rural areas.

One night as I was sleeping with my new "booty call" friend I felt a cold breeze run over me. I shivered and glanced at the window-it was closed and locked. Also, it was summer so where the hell did the cold breeze come from? I did not have AC in my room yet. I gave up trying to solve the mystery and went back to sleep. My booty call woke up and shook me awake and said she heard some strange noises coming from the pipes-like animal sounds… but not quite. The fact she looked concerned sent chills through my whole body. "Maybe it's 'cause the building's so old?" She did not look convinced and glanced around the room cautiously. We held each other tighter and drifted safely off to sleep again. When I woke up again that morning we chit chatted and I kissed her goodbye.

"Hey Kent," I said walking into the living room where he was cooking breakfast with his boyfriend who was the spitting image of John Legend; hot. "Hey Giovanna," he smiled, "Nice hair-you have a good fuck last night?" I laughed, "Yes I did as a matter of fact," and smoothed down my wild copper hair a bit. Kent and I chatted a bit about what we had been up to while his John-Legend lookalike partner did some work on his laptop. "Oh I forgot to tell you!" I put down my tea and dramatically told him the story about the cold breeze and weird noises. "Oh my god!! Last night I had a nightmare about noises in my room! He had to wake me up because I was shaking-literally." "What??" I exclaimed and we spent the next hour analyzing, and overanalyzing what this all meant. It was a bit creepy and unsettling so we decided to drop the conversation and burn some sage. "I have some weed left," Kent smiled naughtily. And we smoked the day away. With each rich sweet tasting inhale-I breathed out the bad and closed my eyes hoping the good was coming in. Kent was always that for me-a reminder of the good that was left in the world when I couldn't see it.

26

5am train rides each day were draining the shit out of me. Plus the dull workdays were becoming more common; sucking the life out of me. I sighed and leaned back against the train seat. I looked around and I realized how much I missed Los Angeles. I closed my eyes and remembered the brief glory days that passed way too quickly. I remember wearing my Dickies with blue 2Pac styled bandanas. Going to the park with my sisters to watch the cute Latino and Black boys play basketball and flirt with my older sister and friends. Listening to music outside the stoop of my home while watching people and cars go by. Sneaking out of my friend's home and hanging with the boys. Those were the days. Santa Monica Blvd, South Central LA, East LA, Cholo crushes, the beach…ahhhh the beach. I could almost feel the sand beneath my feet, smell the salt, and hear the ocean crashing. The train stopped and I opened my eyes to the grim reality. A gloomy toxic city full of people who don't give a damn but none other than themselves. I stood up to get off at my stop and pushed my way through the crowds. I did love NYC but I could barely breathe. I felt like I was dying from lack of oxygen. *Breathe, It is just your ego taking over. Breathe.* I coaxed myself. I leaned over and gasped-trying to catch my breath. The realization that this train car was mostly filled with white men somehow seemed to make things much worse and I grinded my teeth together fighting for equilibrium.

I arrived to work and I felt out of it like always, like I was present in my body but still just hanging around and going through the motions. I was *acting* like a counselor at the school I was employed in and I was *acting* like I knew what I was doing. After I finished work and went straight home, I *acted* like I was ok and was enjoying my weekends. In reality I cried almost every single night. I waited at the edge of my bed for nighttime to hit and stared out the window-contemplating if I should jump out or not. One time I nearly did it while sobbing hysterically, but an unexpected text from Kent stopped me. The text said that he was coming over with the boys to pregame again. Why I happened to look at my phone that exact moment I will never know. All I knew was that it would not be fair for Kent to arrive home to find me splattered in pieces below the window. Plus a child might walk upon my lifeless body. No-I could not do it that way. I cried in frustration. I could not find the perfect way to exit my lifeless life. I turned my phone off and slept.

It reminded me of the quote that talks about humans wearing masks everyday...and didn't Billy Joel sing about that in his song, "Stranger?" Why do we humans feel the need to hide our thoughts, feelings, and emotions? Why do we stifle our souls so that we can live to see another day? Perhaps we do not know who we are. Perhaps it is true that we as a species have lost our way. We do not remember coming from divinity. We do not remember that we are gods and goddesses and should be treated and loved as such.

27

"God that feels good," moaned Marie-the woman I had been casually dating for a couple months. The sex we had was hot and tonight was no exception. We moaned as we rubbed each other waiting for that delicious climax. Marie was Polish and had a heavy accent, which made it quite difficult to read her lips. So we often communicated by texting and writing in person with the occasional ASL she picked up all on her own. "That was a good one," I said after we had come. "Tell me about it baby," she smiled that sexy smile of hers and rolled off of me.

We cuddled and talked a bit about this and that. "So how much can you hear?" she asked. So I explained my level of hearing and what it meant and that it is not the same for another deaf person blah blah blah. The same explanation I give when educating any other hearing person. Don't get me wrong, I love educating people about anything I know, but at times I wish people would care enough to educate themselves. Ever heard of Google?

"That's cool, can you hear this?" clapped Marie. I stared at her in disbelief. "Uhhh…I'm not answering that," I responded carefully.

"Turn around and let me know when you hear something," she persisted. It took all I had to keep the anger from spilling over. I was offended. "Ahem… it's offensive to ask that of a deaf person-whether or not they are hard of hearing." "I'm sorry baby-I'm just curious," Marie apologized and pointed to my ears. "Ok, ummm...I want you to leave. This is not working out for me," I firmly said. Kinda surprised myself by setting down limits. "Are you serious??" she exclaimed. "Yes." She became angry and got dressed quickly and stormed out of my room and apartment. About a couple weeks later she tried to talk to me again. Not happening.

28

After the dealing with Marie, Jonathan was a welcome change. He was mischievous 39-year-old man with fiery red hair. We had met months ago while at a bar with friends. He had come up to me and asked me the signs for "I like bright orange pants." Since he was quirky like that, we hit it off right away laughing and joking about nothing and everything. That night I went home with him and it was maybe the first time in a long time I did not have any flashbacks from my past. It was the first time in a very long time being with a man and not feeling searing pain and anxiety before I felt the pleasure. It actually felt right and good. Muy pleasurable. However, I was still not in any position to be in a serious relationship since I was a mess inside and I knew it very well. No use dragging someone else through the more of my icky feelings of misery. But my feelings for him grew-I could not stifle them. So I tried to end our "thing."

"I'm confused-why are you saying you don't want to see me anymore?" Jonathan asked as we sat on his big green comfortable couch. "Because...I don't want a relationship so what is the point of seeing you if I can't keep my feelings in check? This was not my intention; to develop feelings for anyone." "Me too, me too" he replied, "But I like where this is going. So why not just keep it going how it is and see what happens?"

"But I don't want to-I need to work on myself first," I insisted. He rolled his eyes, "I am a mess too. I am in anger management for heavens sake but sometimes being with someone while we work through our issues is healing." "Hmm…ok-that is a good point." He kissed me and we cuddled on his couch. I was afraid but being with him wasn't so bad-I liked it. *Sooner or later I may need to jump into this ocean*, I decided.

29

"It's been 3 months Giovanna! Why don't you just tell him you want to give a relationship a try? He obviously wants to." Carlis was frustrated because for as long as he has known me I came up with millions of excuses as to why I cannot be in a relationship. He was a hopeless romantic from Ecuador and believes in the best parts of "love." *But what is love? Oh, I gotta listen to Tina Turner's song, "What's Love Got to do With it."*

"I know Carlis but ugh…I don't know!" "Ok-you'll see him tonight after work right? So just go from there and see how you feel." He said and leaned back in his office chair exasperated. "Good idea," and smiled sweetly in a mocking tone. I walked out of his office and down the hall towards mine with a sinking feeling in my stomach, but a small part of me was looking forward to seeing what happened tonight.

My office roommate who I called "the Hippie" was working on an art therapy project so I walked into her office to see what she was up to. She held up a bottle and explained the next steps to create a safe space for children. "That's pretty cool, you'll have to send me the article for that." I said looking over the beautiful artwork. "How's it going with Jonathan?" she inquired. "Well…" I then poured out the whole story about tonight and my childish fears and so on. "Don't let anyone pressure you into a relationship if you're not ready. And only you know if this guy is worth the risk." She gently pointed out. I smiled and we chatted a bit more before we got back to work. *I'll miss my co-workers if I decide to die. They're good people.* I sat down in my chair and looked out the window. Winter was coming, but nothing could be as cold and empty as I was feeling inside. However, I did not know if I even wanted the numbness to thaw out. It might cause an avalanche of feelings and memories I spent so many years trying to forget.

30

"Jonathan," I laughed. I shook my head as he drove up to the curb of where I lived. I laughed because he had one of his silly expressions on. "Ok-I'll be serious now. You look beautiful," he smiled and kissed me. We walked up to the 3rd floor of my apartment and sat down on the couch to have a discussion about "us." "Why are you so afraid of this?" he asked straight out. I then told him some of the reasons such as my parents divorce, lack of relationship role models, independency, and of being hurt. He then took my hands and said, "You are not supposed to know the answers. The process is painful to get to where you want to be but it is worth it. Do not be so hard on yourself." That cut straight to my heart and cracked a wall for some unknown reason and the tears flooded out. "Excuse me," I excused myself and went quickly to my room to collect myself. My face was burning with embarrassment in my little sobbing episode. I had never been so vulnerable in front of a straight man before. "Baby, you ok?" Jonathan walked in and gave me a hug. "I'm so sorry, I don't know why I'm crying." I sputtered. "Good, I am happy you're crying because I can finally *see you*. No wall is up now." That made me cry harder. I sobbed into his shirt and he held me close. I felt safe for a while. "I'll let you think about us some more ok? No pressure. But remember if you saw yourself the way I saw you-you would be flying. You are amazing." I smiled and was speechless. His words were genuine and beautiful. "I love you." He whispered. I stared in disbelief. No sound could come out. Finally I said, "Thanks." *Oy vey.*

31

"*I really like him,*" I texted to my Mum. "*Follow your heart honey. If you feel good about it and he treats you good then there's nothing wrong with trying.*" Part of me felt like my mother supported this because I was dating a man and not a woman. She was convinced that my dating women in the past was just a phase or a political statement. I smiled at this. That was Mum. A small part of me wondered if it was because I had experienced so much trauma with men since I was young that something in my soul shifted. It was like I needed to be with women for a while to heal emotionally and physically/sexually until I could welcome men again. Women were my saving grace in that way. I shook the theories from my mind. *It is not important now*, I convinced myself. "*Ok, I'm gonna jump in and whatever happens happens.*" I texted her back. "*Love ya Mum.*" "*Namastse Giovanna,*" she replied.

"*Hey Jonathan,*" *I wrote anxiously.*
"*Hey there-how are you?*
"*I'm good, I was wondering when you're free to talk?* *I typed back.*
"*I'm pretty busy the next few days at work, everything ok?*" *He asked*
"*Yeah, everything's fine I just want to talk about something whenever you're free. So just text me when you know.*"
"*What is it?*" *He pushed*
"*It's better to talk about this in person-it's good though I promise lol.*" *I assured him*

"God, you're annoying. Just tell me now."

Hurt, I slowly typed that I wanted to give a relationship a try.

Silence.

"I'm not in a position in my life right now to be in a relationship. Especially with someone I really do care about."

My heart sank and sank. "You fucking led me on! I feel so stupid!!! I opened up to you!!" I screamed through my texts.

My heart kept sinking. It wouldn't stop until it crashed to the bottom of my stomach and bled and bled. I started weeping. The parts of me that had become alive again, the parts of me he touched and made me enjoy a little bit more were no longer...once again. I cut a knife through all of the life he planted and uprooted it. I swore I'd never be a fool again. Never again.

32

Slow months passed and I never heard from Jonathan. I never responded to his apology and I never tried to contact him. As far as I was concerned he was a stranger to me. I was filled to the brim with anger. I looked up at the water stained ceiling of my Brooklyn apartment. *Stupid landlord still hasn't fixed the damage*, I sighed. "Hey," Kent walked into my bedroom, "Wanna go out tonight?" "Another gay bar? I need some attention so…" Rolling his eyes he said, "Ok fine, why not gay bar first and then we go to a straight or lesbian bar and get yourself a hot guy or woman?" I smiled slowly spread across my face, "Deal." His smile faded. "You hear that?" he asked slowly and walked over to my wall. I did indeed hear it now-it was faint. Sounded like a toy. "It sounds like a doll laughing-that's *fucking* creepy!" Kent exclaimed. I shuddered and got chills all through my body. There was something dark about this apartment and 'hood. Kent and I spent the afternoon drinking wine and exchanging ghost stories and other things pertaining to the spiritual realm.

"Alright let's go!" I motioned to Kent and we walked out the door to catch the L train to the gay bar. We arrived in about 20 minutes to a raunchy bar with male Go-go dancers on top of the bar table. Of course they were all modern American versions of ancient Greek or Roman gods. Beautifully sculpted bodies and heavenly, manly faces had lust written all over them. I gazed up at one of the dancers and drooled…not literally of course. He looked down at me and gave me a sexy smile and came closer to me. Kent gave me a dollar to put in his underwear so I did…oh lord I did. Kent then accepted a drink from a boy toy and started a flirty conversation with him. The Go-go dancer I was making gaga eyes at had gotten off the table and walked over to me. "It's my break," he then motioned to me to follow him casually. So I discretely followed far behind him to a hidden door. He went in and turned around waiting for me. I walked into the door and he closed it behind us. He grabbed me into his arms and planted a huge kiss on me. He was sweaty and gross…ewww. But still oh so beautiful. We made out and made out.

"Heyyy!" I heard a shout and looked up at 2 bouncers coming through the door. "Out!" one of them yelled at me while the other one reprimanded the Go-go dancer. I played the Deaf card and the Cali card. *Both of those cards together cannot fail*, I told myself and smiled slyly inside. "Excuse me, I can't understand you, I need to read your lips," and motioned to my hearing aids. "Oh," his eyes softened and he became more gentle, "You have to leave, not supposed to be hooking up with the boys."

"What? Really? I'm from Southern CA; I didn't know that was a rule." I looked up at him with my best wide-eyed innocent looking face. "Ok, you can stay. But behave!" he smiled a little and took my hand to lead me out of the room. *That was easy.* Kent saw me and rushed over to me. "What the hell did you do??" I just smiled and giggled. "Take care of yourself ok? You're too beautiful for that shit," the bouncer gently murmured to me and walked back to resume keeping the bar under control…as if that was possible. I then explained to Kent what happened and he guffawed at the fact something like this of course would happen to me at a gay bar!

33

New York City; I love you but you're bringing me down. I saw the quote posted on a friend's Facebook. Exactly what I was feeling EACH DAY. New York City was like a love/hate relationship. Or like a relationship with family-you love your family but more than 3 days with them can cause you to regress to an adolescent and itch to escape from the strongholds. It didn't help that more and more I was missing Southern California; the weather, beaches, vegan food, my CA friends, and the laidback culture, etc. I could go on and on about the pros that outweigh the cons.

I felt stuck and not sure what the next move was. My job was thankless. I had an amazing supervisor and Social Work team BUT the pay was a joke and the parents of the kids I worked with were less than enthusiastic about their own children. And some of the teachers were toxic and cruel. I never imagined I would have a Master's Degree plus a license in my field, and still be struggling financially. I knew I would probably not be at peace with my demons because I could not remember what real peace felt like. *But come on-at least give me some moolah* I often said to no one in particular when I was alone. I often wondered how other countries provided free education, healthcare, and amazing salaries for their people but America couldn't…or won't. It baffled me each time and left me wishing I could move somewhere far away where I thought I'd be happier. Don't they say happiness and peace lie within? Hmm…but what to do if your "within" was numb?

34

"Hi, my name is India," smiled the new Social Work intern sticking out her hand. I smiled back, "Nice to meet you, I'm Giovanna." "Beautiful name!" she gushed. "Look who's talking!" I pointed out and we laughed. India was tall and gorgeous-the kind of gorgeous that makes women insecure and men salivate. I admit I was jealous but that jealousy quickly evaporated because her personality was infectious. We bonded immediately over a shared love of unique tattoos and our CA background. She was intelligent and had the best humor, which helped make each workday bearable. Later we started hanging out after work on the weekends and slowly my love…for NYC came back.

India and I spent the next two years partying, clubbing, smoking weed, and conversing about life. She was like my twin-a much prettier and younger version of myself. I could see myself when I looked at her and it was startling and amusing at times. One night we went to meet with friends at a bar in the hipster part of Brooklyn. *Gags.* Gentrificators, covert racists and cultural appropriators. It was too much to bear so I sipped a beer to wash down the Molly.

"This is my song!" Yelled India and pulled me to the center of the dance floor. I smiled and began dancing and laughing with her. Our friends were in the corner of the bar chatting. It is common in the deaf community to see groups of deaf chatting for hours and hours, even after closing time. I signaled to them to come join us in the midst of this frenzy. The good thing about knowing ASL: you can communicate in any environment, no matter how loud it is. Our friends trekked their way through the tight crowd and joined us. I felt a pair of hands on my right hip, just as another guy pulled India close to him to dance. I turned around and was faced with a very beautiful man. He looked possibly Middle Eastern. Had beautiful wavy black hair, salt and pepper facial hair, dressed immaculately, and eyes that were kind and sexy at the same time. And when he smiled…I became shy and giddy.

"So you do sign language?" Mr. Beautiful asked me. He had a thick accent but luckily I was able to make out what he said…so far. I smiled, "I *know* sign language-not *do*," I corrected him. "Oh, I'm so sorry," he apologized. "No, no, it's ok. We're all learning right?" I said and winked. *I hope I looked really smooth when I winke*d, I thought. "Can I get you a drink?" Mr. Beautiful offered. "Uhh…sure," the Molly was kicking in and I was feeling more and more happy and friendly. He took my hand and led me towards the bar and we squeezed between people to get the bartenders attention. *Why were bartenders usually snobs?* I wondered. "Two beers," he pointed to one of the beers on tap. "Here you go," he handed me mine. "Thanks," I smiled sexily. We then walked to a corner and chatted and chatted and kissed and kissed. Then before I knew it, the bar was closing and India was tapping me on my shoulder. It was time to go.

35

India and I woke up in my bed-the light was peeking through. I rolled over on my side so that we were facing each other. We started giggling like teenagers thinking about last night. We caught up about what happened after we split and I went with Mr. Beautiful. She did the exact same thing I did with her guy; talked and kissed. We gossiped and reminisced about the events, like we were in High School. The worst part of waking up after a great night/ party is that it is a reminder the good never lasts, and that the day seems dull in comparison. I even wrote a silly poem for him during that time:

> "Thank you for your gentleness
> Among all the senselessness
> "Thank you for your sweetness
> Among the bitterness
> Thank you for your wisdom
> When nothing is logic
> And thank you for your love
> For it's magic."

I was sitting outside of my favorite café drinking green tea latte, and reading a mystery book. The book was good, you know the kind that make you feel you are part of the pages and take you on an emotional roller coaster ride. All of a sudden someone tapped me on my shoulder, so I looked up and lo and behold it was Mr. Beautiful. "Uhhh, oh heyyy…" I stammered and took off my chic, oversized sunglasses and attempted to smooth my hair. I had not bothered to put on makeup or wear something overly cute because it was a low key Sunday morning for me. I smoothed out my off the shoulder shirt that said "Los Angeles" on it and attempted to cross my legs to look cute and appealing. "Sorry to startle you," he grinned, "But I hope you remember me?" "Yes, of course I do! Such a small world!" I smiled back at him. I offered for him to join me and he did. We sipped lattes and chatted about nothing and everything.

Mr. Beautiful as it turns out had a real name-Samar. He was a deep thinker, had a conscience, was from a far away country, and his heart matched his looks; beautiful. We exchanged text numbers and agreed to meet up again sometime soon. He had to go to work at an environmental agency, so we hugged bye for now and off we went. Him to work, and I to my apartment to continue my day. As I walked back, I pondered over the events of the day and recent weeks. Perhaps all this hell I have experienced was to help me recognize heaven when it walked by and chatted with me. Heaven in all its glorious forms. Heaven came in the form of laughter, healing, good people, forgiveness, mercy, change, nature, and a stranger's genuine smile. I could go on and on, but thinking so deeply gave me a headache. I needed rest. I arrived home, got into bed for a quick nap and smiled because for a few moments I felt safe in joy.

About a week later Samar texted me and asked me if I wanted to go out on an official date. I said yes and he suggested we meet at his friend's art studio in Manhattan and then go to a nice dinner afterwards. Perfecto. That night of the date I dressed in my best "I can hang with artists, but I'm still Giovanna Black" outfit paired with red lipstick. Since winter was fast approaching, I grabbed a warm coat and scarf and jetted. Off the L train I walked towards the art studio address Samar had given me. I got lost a few times since it was dark and I cannot see well at nighttime, despite the endless trail of streetlights and store lights in Manhattan. Finally I found the dang building where the studio was in. *I'm here finally,* I texted to Samar. *Coming downstairs now* ☒, he texted back. Samar arrived and gave me a big hug and walked me to where the studio was. He introduced me to his friend, Raphael. First thing I noticed besides the gorgeous art studio filled with talented work; Raphael had hearing aids! "Nice to meet you," Raphael said. "You too, I love your work," I gushed looking around. "Well, I can do better, but thank you," and then proceeded to chat with Samar while I looked around artists paradise. I had sketched on and off since I was a little girl, and used to dream of being an artist in Paris living off of café and scones.

After I was done admiring the works, I sat beside Samar and rested my arm on his leg while he continued chatting with Raphael. I concentrated hard on reading their lips to keep up with the conversation. "I think we should wear specific shirts with our logo and then make sure we prepare to be arrested if needed…" I was able to catch Raphael saying. I turned to "read" Samar's response, "Yes definitely, Michael has already been arrested for protesting Wall Street, so we need to be aware and see if his family needs our help too." Then more talk of politics ensued, and the Civil Rights Movement was mentioned as well as the Black Power Movement. "You know, I am not sure if marching or protesting will change things anymore. It's a different era and people respond to different things now. Yes, taking it to the streets and letting the people make the change is the "Marx" way of doing things, but…I dunno." I shook my head thoughtfully. Samar grinned at me and put his hand on my knee, "Yes, we don't know if it will change things, but we see improvements, so it does work in some ways. We have to keep trying."

After about an hour of talking we said bye to Raphael and thanked him for letting us see his studio. Samar and I walked to a nearby restaurant to eat dinner since we were famished. He ordered a beer and I ordered one too. Since I began taking anti-anxiety medication my tolerance for alcohol was even more low than usual, so I could never finish a full glass of beer but I always tried. We ordered food and while we waited for it to arrive, we chatted and sipped our beer. After a while I was buzzed. "I can't drink anymore," I pushed the barely sipped beer in his direction, "finish it for me," I smiled ruefully. "You know, you don't have to force yourself to try or to feel obliged to order alcohol. Just be yourself," Samar said and massaged my shoulder gently. I smiled a bit, "Alright Mr. Perfect, anything you need to tell me?" I laid my hand over his. "Yes, actually uhh…I'm married," he nervously said. My face fell. What the hell? Not again. "No no, wait," he laughed nervously, "Your face," he continued laughing. "Ok, seriously, we are in the process of getting divorced, but we wanted to wait until she got back on her feet. I promise you that we do not even live together," he proceeded to show me a bunch of texts between them that confirmed what he just told me. I hit his arm, "You scared me!" I laughed in disbelief. "I know, I'm sorry," Samar looked at me with those dreamy, dark soulful eyes and gave me a soft kiss on my cheek. *Sighs*. Bliss.

36

Weeks and months passed. I avoided Samar every single day and tried to get him out of my head every single second. Why- of course you may ask? Because I was scared. All of my emotional baggage spilled out of my wounds, and I couldn't clean up the mess. I had not cut myself in years, so it was as if all of the sadness and anger had built up in my blood and needed to be drained. It was like trying to clean up a gallon water spill with a square of toilet paper. And I did not know what to do when the nightmares came again, I did not know how to let it out without physically cutting open my veins. The other night I had dreamed that I picked up a screwdriver and wanted to stab the other guy who hurt me when I was a kid because I was so angry. I couldn't speak my anger in the dream because no one believed me, so instead I resorted to violence. I tried to kill the memory, but it continued to invade my dreams. And I feared Samar would turn out to be just like every other asshole. Samar, poor guy, was left in the dark, but being the human being he is-he let me go and wished me well.

37

I fell into a deep depression again for about an year. I hid it well because I did not want pity. I just wanted people to think everything was fine and dandy until somehow my time came, and I could discretely bury myself into the ground under my headstone. In fact, every time I passed a cemetery I imagined how peaceful it must feel to just be gone-a ghost. To sleep forever. To shed the body I love but that has been violated a few times too much. Sometimes I wanted to just sneak away at night and go to the cemetery, just to lay there until death overcame me.

I missed Samar. I missed his smile and his kind eyes. His sexiness, his wisdom, and his peace. He was sanity in this crazy world. He was air when I couldn't breathe, because of the anxiety weighing on my chest. I picked up my phone and debated for a few minutes; *Should I text him? Should I not? What's the point? What if he doesn't respond?? Argh!* I put my phone away in my purse and walked home from work. It was a somewhat sunny but chilly day. I closed my sweater around me tighter and I realized, *It was time for me to return to CA*. I needed the beach, the warmth, and the dry air. I needed the mountains, the palm trees and the space for my claustrophobic self to grow. I grew tired of NYC. Or maybe it was the fact that in NYC it was immensely crowded, so much that one could not escape. The crowds and the endless distractions never bothered me so much until now. Maybe I was not tired of NYC, maybe I was tired of running from my thoughts and the ghosts that shadowed me everyday? I couldn't stay to find out I had told myself. I just had to find a way out of this place for good.

38

Time. What to make of it? Well, all I knew was that 4 years had passed of me being and working in NYC. I was done. I had reached my limit and was crying out internally for the beach, sun, and all that made CA what it is. NYC had also raised my anxiety level to the extremes, to the point where the 1st time in my life I needed daily medication. I had secretly been applying to jobs nationally, with focus on CA. As a couple years went by, I began to share my plans with people. Some didn't take me seriously, and some wished me well. So finally in my 4th year I received a job offer and was beyond thrilled. It felt like maybe this time I'd be rescued. I cannot explain it. However, I just knew that this time I would return to California was to *live*, not die. I owe that to my friends and family, and especially my students who unknowingly and unintentionally showed me light that banished my own darkness.

I found a therapist who knew ASL and went to her weekly. She was an Earth Angel, as Doreen Virtue, the author, would say. It was a safe haven for me in a suspicious, violent, and sick world. It was tough for me to be attached to her since I knew any second or minute it could all change. There are no guarantees in this life. But I went and I dug deep. Most of the gunk I was able to get out, about my suicidal tendencies and attempts but not about that specific man. Most of the memories were blocked and I knew if they were unleashed I would unravel in a very bad way. Possibly to the point of no return 6 feet under by my own hand.

The more I went to therapy, the more I grew in a positive way. The growth was utterly painful, but I began to love myself in a way I did not know how to previously. I began to stop relying or wishing others could protect me. I began to protect myself and believe I was indeed worth it, just like every other human being. Old Giovanna began to die. I did not know that girl anymore. She died and died a violent death. Now someone was being reborn again and the song of the siren this time is a hopeful one filled with untainted love. This woman I am now birthing is one who is scarred but healed, broken but whole, and there I stand again and again. Alive.

39

Driving on the 405 with the windows down. Paradise. So relieved to be back where I was born and raised. *To live and die in LA.* 2pac said it all. I turned up the music louder until it vibrated in my ears and through my whole body. I was driving to meet a date from online and was a wee bit nervous, but excited. His name was Wendell and he was an engineer from Florida, who moved to CA solely for work. I parked in the lot of the café and locked my car doors after I got out and adjusted my cute outfit. And there he was, Wendell, looking handsome and sharp in his crisp outfit. "Hey" he smiled at me and we hugged briefly. Right away I could tell he was a charmer and was used to getting what he wanted. He might as well have been a lawyer. Seems he could talk or smile his way out of anything.

Once seated inside the café we flirted and talked about our backgrounds and other mundane stuff and flirted some more. "Wanna go back to my place? I promise we don't have to do anything." He asked and gave a charming smile. I agreed. "Yeah sure, and we'll see if I don't have to do anything," I smiled and tried to tease. It worked because he took my hand to pull me in and kissed me-hot. A small part of me was whispering; *He's a stranger! You don't know what he's capable of!* I ignored it and convinced myself that I knew what I was doing and that I was reading him correctly; harmless.

Wendell lived in the beautiful part of Hollywood and had a big ass place that was gorgeous! It was too modern for my taste but still I appreciated the luxury. We kissed and had amazing sex. He knew how to use his body and hands, which sent me over the edge multiple times. "Let's have some wine," he gasped as we tried to catch our breath. He rolled out of bed and came back with an expensive looking bottle. He handed it to me and I gulped it down and we took turns. I was drunk as fuck. Since I wasn't falling or blacking out I thought it was ok. A-ok. We fucked some more and some more until I finally realized it was very late and I had work the next day. So I cleaned myself up a bit and put my clothes back on. "I had fun, you're so beautiful," Wendell said as he looked into my eyes. "Me too," I grinned. I left. And as soon as I stepped into my car, a huge wave of nauseous came up. I gagged and quickly opened the car door and threw up rich purple liquid. Wine. "Damn it." I sat in my car until I felt sober and less nauseous. I then started my car and drove back home and for some reason felt lonely.

40

"You've caught me in your web," Wendell said jokingly, "I can't stop thinking about you. You must've done something to me." I just laughed, "Believe me, I did nothing. Nada. Zip." Wendell shook his head and kissed me on my cheek. We saw each other every week for the next three months. On the fourth month I met a bunch of his close friends from college at a bar. "Hiii!" a peppy, beautiful woman with blonde hair approached me with a wide smile. "Hi," I smiled back and she hugged me enthusiastically. "I've heard a lot of great things about you Giovanna. I'm Bonnie." "Nice to meet you Bonnie, I have heard about you as well. You and Wendell went to college together right?" She nodded, and took a sip of her wine and went into extensive and humorous detail about how they met. I sipped my beer and listened to her and nodded when appropriate, but was becoming exhausted from reading lips.

"Psst, I'm gonna have to leave soon. Remember I mentioned lip reading being exhausting, well it's happening now." "I'm not leaving without you, stay for a little bit," he begged. "Ok, a few more minutes," I smiled slightly and went back to drinking my beer and struggling to read lips of everyone who introduced themselves to me and inquired about my background and my "relationship" with Wendell. I glanced at Wendell and watched as he oozed charm, that's one thing I liked about him but he was a self-admitted flirt. Big time. I went back to my conversation about nothing and everything, then noticed that Wendell was flirting with the bar tender and looking at her cleavage as she threw her head back dramatically obviously trying to charm him too. *Fucking bitch*, I muttered to myself. I stormed over to Wendell, "I'm leaving now," and forced a smile. I hugged everyone who was still left bye and made my way towards the exit.

He grabbed my arm just before my foot touched the doorframe. "What was that?" He demanded to know. "I told you 30 minutes ago I was exhausted, I can barely keep up with the conversations now. And now you're busy flirting." I raised my voice. "Hey, I can't help if I'm amazing," he joked. Part of me fell for his charm again and the other part of me was filled to the brim with fury. I turned around again and attempted to leave. "Come on, I am not letting you go home by yourself. We were supposed to leave together," he insisted. "No, I can't right now." And I walked out fully aware that even though he was wrong, I was the bitch too. *But isn't it degrading to call myself and another woman that word? Well it could also be empowering, taking back the word*. I tried to convince myself and pondered over my thoughts while I walked to the train.

When I finally got off on my stop an hour later, I felt my phone vibrate in my Eco-friendly jacket pocket. *I don't understand what just happened. Everyone is watching me be upset and trying to console me*, the text from Wendell read. Pangs of guilt arose in me and I paused to respond, *I'm sorry I left but you have to understand where I'm coming from*. Sent. I continued walking to my apartment with my phone in my hand, I felt another text come through but waited until I was actually in my apartment and cozy to respond. I opened the door and changed out of my cute clothes and washed my face. Once I felt better and made a cup of green tea, I picked up my phone again and read his message, *I know baby, and I love you. Why don't you come over to my place and we fuck each other's brains out*. I…I didn't know what to say to that. Part of me was repulsed, but I felt so shitty for how things turned out, like I should've been nicer to him for no good reason. *Ok, I'm on my way*, I typed. How'd did it come to this? It was raining outside.

41

Wendell and I didn't work out. Big surprise-ha. I decided to listen to my gut instinct for once in my life as my therapist in the past had encouraged me to keep practicing. I broke it off with him and surprisingly (note sarcasm) felt lighter. Looking back I realized that I hid a lot of his negatives from people such as his tendency to drink in huge proportions of whiskey daily, his constant flirting with women and blaming his "personality" on it. I could go on and on-but at the time I chose to see his light and his potential. *Why'd I feel the need to protect him? Why did I feel the need to not mention anything bad? It was a fucking pattern with me.* Always seeing the potential in people and believing they can change if they wanted to. As I walked to the park near my apartment, I pondered over my life and relationship patterns with men. Pain and heartbreak is unavoidable, but how much is self-induced? How much is from our fathers? How much of it is a result of our own twisted thinking that we deserve it and "that's just the way it goes." *No, this can't be true.* I sat under a Weeping Willow in the park and debated within myself if it was possible to find "true love," or is that all just hype and fiction driven by a male dominated world for exploitation?

In the distance was a father playing softball with his son-at least I assumed that was his son. I sat and watched them for a while, feeling a few bursts of joy at the seemingly good relationship I saw in front of me. I felt my phone vibrate. I took it out of my pocket and saw I had a message from my Mum; *just checking in.* I smiled and then swiped over to my FB page and in my newsfeed I saw *him.* It was an old picture of Ben with friends of mine when they were in college. Someone-one of my current friends to be exact- commented on it…my own friend commented on this picture. She said; *"This was one of the most fun times in my life. Wish we could all do that again." She knows what happened with us in college. She knows that night messed me up to the core. What the hell??* Rage filled me, then sadness, and then just pure hurt. I felt alone. More alone than ever. I wanted to scream. Then I began second guessing myself about whether that night was my fault or not. But I knew deep down it was NOT my fault. I don't give a shit if I was drunk or not-he did NOT have my consent. I wanted to text her and ask her to FT with me, to ask what was she thinking?? But I knew that would be futile. Survivorcentric?? Yeah right. She was such a hypocrite. Tears welled up in my eyes, and I got up quickly so no one could see me and walked quickly back to my apartment.

I opened the door to my apartment, walked in and fell to my knees and wept. I think I must have cried for about an hour, because when I finally peeled myself off of the floor and looked out the window, it was dark. I tried to talk myself out of the depression that was slowly impending upon me. I looked around for positive quotes to "talk" away the negative thoughts. It was like I was fighting tooth and nail against myself and it felt like a losing battle. *Hope is exhausting*, someone once said. I decided to try music, so I grabbed my laptop and put my hearing aids on. I listened to some classical music and then decided to write a bit. As I was writing my eyes began pouring heavy teardrops. I don't know what I was crying for this time, but it felt like a purging and that I could make it through the night.

"It's like I took the knife and sliced the night sky
Heaven poured out its thunder and stars
I swallowed them all so that my spirit could be warm and constantly reborn."

42

"Ghosts don't haunt us. That's not how it works. They're present among us because we won't let go of them."-Sue Grafton. The quote resided with me-I read it over and over again in the book until I became sleepy. I turned onto my side and looked at the time; 8pm. *So early, but so tired.* I had work the next day and was not exactly looking forward to it. I leaned back into my peach colored satin pillow and sighed. A million thoughts shot through my mind, causing a headache that threatened to spiral into a migraine. I tried to meditate and focus on my breathing, but the pain surged like a steak knife through my brain. It reminded me of that ripping feeling between my legs. I grimaced in pain and curled up into a fetal position. *No way medicine was gonna stop this one.* So I let the thoughts flow. And they did flow like rivers of toxic waste that needed to be cleaned out until it was all clear again.

"*Gramps died last night,*" the text on my phone from my Mum read. I sat up from my bed in shock. I was wide awake now. The migraine had disappeared, but now my whole body was a migraine. Especially my heart. I sobbed. Gramps was *not* a perfect father to my Mum and her brothers, BUT he grew and changed, so that when he became my grandfather I only knew the good mostly. He was a person of integrity and dignity-that was the best way to describe him. Now that he was gone, I felt alone. I felt like the good women and men were dying out and leaving us with the bad apples. I did not feel safe-I wanted my Gramps back. I pulled myself out of bed and looked at the time. *Fuck, I had work. Well, then again seeing my students always made me smile.* So I stepped in the shower and attempted to keep my head up, but it bowed and the tears spilled. "*Remember the good,*" he always said. I stepped out of the shower and finished getting ready. I felt heavy-like I was carrying 2x my weight.

"I am so sorry about your grandfather," my coworkers said. "Let me know if you need anything," others said. "Go home Gia and rest," my supervisor said. I know I should be home but I wanted to see my students, they needed me I thought. However, after seeing my 3rd student, I could not stop the tears from coming, so I had to go home. And I did. At home I mulled over the emails he wrote me and the cards he sent. I texted with my Mum back and forth as well to be sure she was ok. I talked to my sisters a bit too.

"*In the middle eighties, Grammy and I and a couple that were close friends spent about six or seven days in London (an inexpensive hotel near the rail station --Enrico's and about a week on a narrowboat north of London. The cities that were beginning and end of the canal trip were Fradley Junction and Stoke On Trent.*" I smiled and reminded myself to book a trip there in the future. One of the last emails to me read;

> "*When one looks at the way almost everything in nature gets older. Much the same way. The equipment that moves the liquids around don't work very well and so things begin to wilt and dry out. The colors that start out so bright and attractive get duller and yet in a way they look sort of "proper". Maybe the right thing to do is to watch the rose for a while yet.*"

I could not stop crying. I mulled over death and what it's purpose was. A myriad of different theories. But I, I believe no one ever really dies. All are transformed into what we need to be. The ones who remain resistant or traumatized are ghosts until they are able to see the light.

The nightmares returned again and again. I woke up one morning with my hands around my neck. I was choking myself. My anger had consumed me and turned me against myself. I had no way of lashing out at life, perpetrators, bullies and racists from HS, etc. etc. so I subconsciously lashed out at myself instead. Waking up with my hands around my own neck was disturbing. I burned sage constantly and that made me feel better, but I forgot that when you remove the bad, you need to invite the good in. I never did that, so I was constantly left with empty spaces that my ghosts from the past willingly filled. It was like a cavity that is cleaned out, the dentist needs to fill it in order for it to heal or else decay sets in. Plus, I was constantly woken up to something touching my arm and legs and waking up to find no one there. No one was there, because I could not see.

It was all too much, so I got my good ol' blade out. I stood looking at a mirror; I put down the blade and realized my search for heaven was futile because it was already in me-it was in my hands. I glanced down at the blade and threw it in the trash. I sobbed quietly and sank to the floor. I pulled my knees up to my chest and a feeling of peace slowly glided over me. It was as if a cloud of witnesses surrounded me at that moment. My Mum always spoke of them and this time I knew what she meant. I felt my sisters, Mum, Grandma, Papa, Grammy, Gramps, cousins, good friends from the California university, my dear niece's loving divine energy, and my former therapist. I had already died multiple times and now it was time for me to allow rebirth. To allow myself to feel what it's like to love and be loved. I stood up, walked to my car and drove all the way to Joshua Tree Park; right into the heart of what was to me the High Desert. I got out and climbed the highest rock I could, and there I scanned the beautiful stillness. Finally the last patch of anger and sadness melted. My ghosts went to the light, and my demons died and this time I felt it and smiled; I am alive:

"The world will hurt you
But sweetheart, you don't have to burn
Collect your hurts from those fires
And bury them in your home
They will be eaten by the soil and the sun
And that is how wars within are won."